WALL STREET BONDS

The Urban Renaissance

TERRENCE L. GALLMAN

ISBN-9781790251780

TABLE OF CONTENTS

DEDICATION

There is no doubt in my mind that this work would not have been done without the constant motivation from my kids, family, and friends and the courage of my colleagues who prioritize our communities above themselves.

INTRODUCTION

For far too long Americans have allowed themselves to be persuaded that the government's job is to take care of them: feed them, clothe them, house them, educate them, raise their children, heal their infirmities, manage their finances, protect them from their own enemies, guard them against all dangers (real and imaginary), and provide for their every need. The point at which they go wrong is in failing to recognize that there's always a catch to such a devil's bargains, purportedly carried out for the good of all the society.

You want free education for your children? The government can take care of it but in exchange, your children will be molded and indoctrinated into compliant, obedient citizens, who reflect the government's values rather than your own.

You want free health care? The government can take care of that too but in exchange your medical decisions and how you live and die will ultimately be determined by corporations. To these corporations you are little more than a line item impacting their profit and loss margins.

You want to be insulated from all things that might cause offense? That's not a problem for the government as the police will use hate crime laws to criminalize speech, thought and actions that may be politically incorrect.

You want a guarantee of safety? Sure, but your local police will also have to be militarized and trained in battlefield tactics, your communities and communication subjected to round-the-clock surveillance, and you—the citizenry—will be treated as suspects and enemy combatants.

You want to root out domestic extremism and terrorism? That's just fine but in the process of identifying and targeting terrorists, the government will have the power to label anyone who disagrees with its policies as an extremist/terrorist, and subject them to indefinite detentions.

Getting the picture?

This is the terrible price the loss of our freedoms and the enslavement of future generations, who will eventually pay for the goods and services rendered by a government whose priorities are the acquisition of more power, control and money.

An old adage warns that a government big enough to give you everything you want is a government big enough to take away everything that you have. Unfortunately, we've been on the receiving end of the government's taxpayer-funded handouts—and its deceptively well-intended dictates for so long that many Americans have forgotten what it is like to think for themselves, provide for themselves, and govern themselves. Indeed, in an age of entitlement it is a far cry from the previous cries by the founders of the constitution.

Gone is the proud, independent-minded, pioneering spirit of early Americans who like my parents rejected what they called 'hand-outs' and worked hard for whatever they had. They also protected their homes and families and believed the government's job was to govern based on the consent of the governed and not to dictate. Contrasting this school of thought by the early Americans who took to heart James Madison's admonition to trust all those in power, with today's citizens who not only expect the government to take care of their needs but have also blindly entrusted the government with excess powers, we observe the weak links.

By giving the government the green light to act in loco parentis and treat the citizenry as children in need of caretakers, we the people allowed ourselves to be demoted and infantilized, reduced from knowledgeable, independent-minded, capable masters of a republic to wayward, undisciplined, dependent, vulnerable children incapable of caring for ourselves.

It's time to grow up!

Incredibly, despite the fact that we allowed the government to become all-knowing, all-powerful and all-mighty, in the mistaken belief that it would make our lives safer, easier and more affluent, we're still shocked when that power and might is used against us. It's time to stop being so gullible and trusting.

Even when the headlines blare out the news about SWAT team raids gone awry, police shootings of unarmed citizens, roadside cavity searches of young women, children being shackled and tasered, and Americans jailed for profit in private prisons; we still somehow maintain our state of denial. A state that is awakened when suddenly we're the ones in the firing line being treated like suspects and criminals, having our skulls cracked, our doors smashed, our pets shot, our children terrorized, and our loved ones jailed for non-offenses.

It's time to remove those rose-colored, partisan-tinted glasses and wake up to the fact that this nation of sheep, has given rise to a government of wolves.

Even though deep down we have suspected that the system is run by an elite group, who view the citizenry as little more than cattle destined for the slaughterhouse, we're still shocked to find ourselves treated like slaves and economic units.

How could we not have seen it coming? How long has the writing been on the wall? How could we have been so blind, deaf and dumb to the warnings all around us? Unfortunately, this happens with each age and in every place where freedom falls and tyranny flourishes.

As Aldous Huxley recognized in his foreword to Brave New World, '*A really efficient totalitarian state would be one in which the all-powerful executive of political bosses, and their army of managers control a population of slaves who do not have to coerced, because they love their servitude. To make them love it, is the task assigned, in present-day totalitarian states, to ministries of propaganda, newspaper editors and schoolteachers.*' This is how the seeds of authoritarianism are planted and watered and cultivated into aggressive, invasive growths that can quickly dominate an environment.

Remember, tyrants don't always come to power in a show of force. Often, they sweet-talk their way to absolute power, buoyed along by a wave of populist demand for someone to save the country from economic, military and political crises.

SETTING THE STAGE

Africa the world's richest continent in resources, has been projected by the EMPEA and IFC World Bank Group as positioned to overtake the U.S., China, and India as the new world economy by 2050.

Though saddled with humanitarian crises, several financial advancements targeting the unbanked are observable. For example, MasterCard Foundation in their financial inclusion strategy are engaged in a series of partnerships (public-private, private and non-governmental organizations), aimed at impacting millions of Kenyans financially. Further, they have partnered with the Kenyan government in the infamous 'huduma number' that was targeted at providing a single window access to citizens for services with the backdrop of promoting youth enterprises to accelerate economic development. Besides the initiatives by MasterCard Foundation, another landmark advancement in the continent has been the M-Pesa system in Kenya. M-Pesa is the brainchild of Safaricom PLC and was launched in 2007 and has gained nationwide acceptance becoming the most utilized platform for virtual money transfer.

The world's digital footprint portends a future for cellphones considering an upsurge in the number of users, and today the three billion mark forecasted globally has been surpassed. Further it is estimated by Statista that 59% of the global population are active internet users who spend a significant amount of time on their cellphones. It is this level of progression that serves as a leader in economic empowerment and inclusion, more so on electronic financial transactions through smartphones. Notwithstanding the downsides of cashless transactions, a decrease in crime and its prevention have also been recorded as a benefit.

It is such concepts, which support the surge in prepaid accounts in the United States, e.g. RushCard, American Express, Green Dot etc., as banks increase their offer on basic cards. However, the American market is not continually engaging and there is evidently an overflow of cash from the black-market rule. This grey area needs to be addressed to increase the flow of funds and attract investment for the community, because as the community develops so will investment opportunities. The impact of this growth will be a subsequent growth in civic engagement through voting, representation at local developments, and organizing of events targeting increased business inclusion. Addressing the pain areas will also help redirect income that continues to trickle out through criminalization, drug use, money laundering, tax evasion etc., back into the community.

Business moguls, e.g. Leap Frog, Bloomberg, JP Morgan, Morgan Stanley, Franklin Templeton and Goldman Sachs are today fixated in creating investments opportunities, a drive that has been realized in global economic forums and conferences where data, insights and research are deliberated and actioned. Additionally, technology continues to take center-stage in facilitating inclusion and empowering the financial sector.

The byproduct of these financial empowerment and inclusion forums, is perceived in the reduction of crime in communities. For instance, cashless transactions reduce the exchange of cash, leading to the plummeting of robberies and extortion. On the other hand, electronic transactions provide a paper trail enabling tracking.

Urban communities are in the purview of high statistics in crime due to challenges present in the implementation of electronic transactions. The lack of engagement relationships between these communities and financial companies besides direct deposits received from their employment, is one facilitating factor of this state of being.

Financial institutions are not observed to engage actively urban industries e.g. entertainment, clubs, and sporting events, where most of these communities make the bulk of their leisure transactions and are more likely to start their own businesses. In any case, a huge number of small vendors still operate in cash in spite of the likelihood of counterfeit money. Therefore, the unbanked population continues to operate away from financial innovations that enhance tracking. Operating in an indeterminate state makes taxation difficult.

Though members of these urban communities access government jobs in industries such as jails and prisons, there is not much innovation that can expand their investment opportunities. Besides this fact, the communities are not likely to benefit from the other job prospects they seek, thus end up relying on private funding, philanthropy and donors to fund social and economic programs in their communities. Considering the influx of people dependent on these jobs, the community is also bound to suffer even as more money is pumped into the system for fear of public outcry and protest.

Pumping more money into the system ignores the concept of prevention as a necessity, thus our goal is to empower organizations in these communities to embrace, and aid in implementing preventative strategies.

High crime rate within the urban community, though not the entire populace participates in criminal activities, remains the reason for missed investment opportunities within the community. Investors have to contend with lack of systems to track revenue, leading to the business unattractiveness in the environment. Ultimately, this leads to businesses struggling to meet their basic needs in the short and long-terms. Additionally, the effort of foreign business owners within the community is harbored by the inabilities of the populace, leading to discrimination.

Most businesses including government industries and organizations, remain unaware that their lack of progressive aggression towards addressing these economic challenges, support an increase in criminal activities discouraging investment. This state of ignorance is at the backdrop of studies indicating that 70% of thefts are employee related. Business performance is then exposed to an already broken social service sector, increasing the cost of doing business within a community that serves as its customer base.

The fact that most businesses avoid the urban communities leads to over saturation of businesses in the more modern communities. The resulting effects are inflation, higher costs, higher taxes and eventually deflationary periods, fall in goods, services, and prices. Further the community adapts and seeks investments that settle their retirement and or cost of living resulting to opportunities emerging only within their need. Though this is significant, there is a lack of the ability to erect institutions that diversely support the community and help generate wealth through the available pool of talent, energy and resources in the community.

Another concentrated effort is within the criminal justice system, lobbying firms and investment make up. If you look at the public traded company portfolio, in comparison with the basic investment it takes to produce a tax paying citizen and the difference in investment, a solution to the ills affecting the community can be identified. An individual who is invested in the community and paying taxes within their basic income, contributes to the economy compared to one who is discriminated against and living below poverty standards, with an inheritance of all associated ills of crime, poor health and lack of inclusion, who cannot make ends meet costs the economy more. This is because the talent is not set up for productivity and efficiency though requiring space and care.

The cost associated with reforms on crime is estimated at 500 billion. Considering that 2.5 million adults are incarcerated, the reality is that the possible 33% on a basic income of 40k, could easily restore civility but cannot be accessed. I remember seeing a 1999 prospectus of the Federal Bureau of Prison Industries (UNICOR) which made an estimation on the number of employees they would have focusing on inmates in a span of 10 years.

Laws and politics arise from politicians who seek public support, and often the true measure of their effort is constrained by new and more aggressive campaigns e.g. George Bush 'Say no to ending parole for nonviolent offenders', Clinton Anti-Terrorism Bill that put 100k law enforcement in the black community amongst others. All these affect community politics, newspaper articles, TV press and emotional sentiments, setting the tone for events, attractions and community investment into the industries that urban communities spend their time, energy and limited resources to make a return or leverage on investments.

The politics of crime comes from the city managers, mayors, councils, elected officials, chief of police, staff, coroners etc. It is driven during the setting up of budgets, agendas, and distribution of wealth and resources. Ordinances and or enforcements often dictate the flow of investments, resources, and funds that may not support industries in urban communities or the urban community itself.

Many organizations, volunteers and institutions are guided to development, with prevention of criminality often the subject of discretionary discrimination. Elements arising from this subject come from the Bill of Rights, Constitution, The Rule of Law, and Magna Carta which serve as the drivers for town hall protests, and the lack of civility in public places. My journey to trace and change the course of this discourse would be an awful long and arduous one but not without some great vindication and rewards.

My journey started in prison with a renegade Hispanic counselor named Cortez and a group of disgruntled inmates who had more time on their hands to take advantage of an existing opportunity within the credit for courses system. The inmates attained a lower security classification for programming according to the security classification codes, since they were forced to take one class offered by the prison every six months. The prison staff took rotations to help keep the inmates engaged and the entire population under a watch. In turn recommendations were made to the unit team consisting of a Counselor, Case Manager and Unit Manager who offered a classification stating whether an inmate could be sent to a lower classification. Based on your offense, level one could be sent to Super-max (hosted worse misconduct) or to a camp adjacent to a military base. The camp had no fences or walls and the only thing that kept an inmate incarcerated, was the threat of an additional 5 years and being sent back behind the fence or walls, with the duration to be spent dependent on the time and energy spent in getting one back into custody. The fact that we were at a low custody facility and only one fence away from camp status motivated us to take up programs even if it meant learning nothing and being taught nothing. This arrangement made lower classification of an inmate a big deal since it meant less security.

It didn't really matter to us what we were doing besides the focus on being sent to lower custody status through the program. This was the same attitude visible among the staff instructors who approached the program the easiest possible way. Most counselors would just throw up their hands at the slightest resistance and say, 'Hey! you guys live here 24 hours a day 365 days a year. Now multiply that by the number of years you will be here.' The duration ranged between months to over 20 years. However, Counselor Cortez always asked us to sign up for financial literacy class.

A financial literacy class sounded better than the other classes that were offered such as anger management and accounting. I thought accounting was a joke because who was going to let a convict count their money, and what could you learn about accounting over a course period of six weeks? Some of the inmates who took up accounting thought they could get a job in accounting using the certificate, regardless of their background check. More so the length of some of our sentences were so long that the papers would be useless at the end of serving our time. I was among these inmates, but hopelessly remained optimistic and inspired, in any case the choices were limited.

The lessons were held in a staff member's office with a makeshift seating arrangement for six or seven inmates. Most of us spent an hour or so gazing around the room at the staff's personal pictures - their kids and family - which were intended to help us focus on the good in us. However, this often made us view them negatively. The few certificates of recognition awarding them as great corrections team members, kept us thinking about their rewards emanating from keeping us locked up and preoccupied. I learned that there is good and bad in everything, and it all depends on how much time is available.

Cortez was good at keeping us focused on him through sharing with us how each course was improving his personal life and making him stand out from other staff doing the same thing within the correctional system. The class started with an introduction that included him advising us that this was not beneficial to his own life, as he emphasized how he was breaking prison protocol – we thought he wanted a pat on the back from us. Later I discovered that he was struggling financially to make ends meet as a security guard and counselor.

Needless to say, by bringing in a 12-week cd course of Rich Dad Poor Dad by Robert Kiyosaki, Counselor Cortez taught us everything we didn't know about money. Money we did not have now and with our current status we had no chance of making. These basic truths about our state of being did not change the fact that the course opened us up to truths on why most urban inmates were incarcerated in the first place. Most of us were born to financially illiterate families, and lacked access to proper housing, education, and any form of social inclusion, due to discretionary discrimination which I will explain later in this book.

While this course was a good place to start it was a long way from being our salvation. However, the main takeaway from the course was that while *we may not have been all of our problem, we had to become our own solution.*

The course led me to take more courses focused on learning about money and finance, not just for the lower classification but also to secure my financial independence – the very reason for my imprisonment. This course proved right away that *a person who is financially illiterate doesn't know what to do with money when they get it,* just like the Bible says - a fool and his money shall depart. Looking back at my life, I had gone one way and my money had taken the other way. I had to start somewhere and there was no better time and place than where I was. Besides, cameras show up way before the results come in.

The next course was on 'value addition' which I was taught in the company of two inmates who were poised to create a pipeline from Europe across the USA. They may have either robbed Koch brothers or were on to something good, but either way they had a great work ethic though no one believed them. My takeaway from the course was that *I needed to find a stream of revenue, put myself in the middle and add value to myself while accumulating wealth.* The courses paved my way to a less secure prison camp.

Up until the late 1990s most camps were designated for white collar crimes e.g. tax evasion, and banking related. These were similar to Paul Manafort and Rich Gates charges in the Muller investigation, and the investigation of President Trump's senior campaign official. Since the penalties for white collar crimes had become more severe, most of the higher security institutions held more of these inmates, and I was able to expand on my financial information by networking with these tech and financial professionals. After several years of learning and networking I was awarded a certificate by the AITFM (American Institute of Trading the Financial Markets).

AITFM was created as a platform to help educate people, particularly in the urban community to learn about trading and how to trade the financial markets. Profoundly, to date only one black female works on the floor of the New York Stock Exchange.

Studying at AITFM helped me through a myriad of financial establishments, e.g. Angel and Venture Capitalists investment groups, Atlanta and Southeast Angel groups, New York and upper East Coast Yale Clubs private funding etc. This was in addition to attending panels with Gavin Serkin, sharing a stage at the IFC Global Private Equity Conference in DC where global trillion dollar investor institutions (such as Goldman Sachs, Morgan Stanley, World bank Group, Black Rock, Government Pensions funds from Japan, United States, Security Exchange Commission, Bill and Melinda gates Foundation, BlackRock Private Equity Partners, Leap Frog Investments) congregate, to books such as Wall Street Bonds (a cautiously optimistic approach to bind the two extremes of philanthropy and institutional investment, to help transform the uncharted impact of social and financial inclusion for economic development through urban America).

The success and economic growth of these institutions are intrinsically intertwined, and capable of addressing human needs and concerns related to poverty, crime health, and prosperity. This is attainable through innovation and invention of solutions embedded within these needs.

THE IRISHMAN, THE SOUTH CAROLINIAN, AND THE ENGLISHMAN INTERNATIONAL THOUGHT LEADERS PANEL DISCUSSION AT NEWBERRY COLLEGE 2015

The International Thoughts Leaders Conference and Panel discussion in 2015 at Newberry College with Gavin Serkin, and Vincent Coyle

The conference was opened by Professor, Dr. Peggy Winder's, a National Diversity Award winner. In the opening remarks she stated that the dialogue would no doubt break down economic barriers, support financial inclusion initiatives and inform justice and reconciliation.

Gavin Serkin's on the other hand started by telling a joke about an Irishman, a South Carolinian, and an Englishman. He said that no one knew where our relationship would go or the punch line to our new mission. The room was filled with laughter because of the diversity of our backgrounds, not to mention our accents. As the

Head of Bloomberg International Desk of Emerging Markets in London, fresh off the publication of his book *Frontier: Exploring the Top 10 Emerging Markets of Tomorrow* by Bloomberg and Wiley Finance, he had spent the previous three years traveling to over 60 countries mainly Africa, Asia, Europe, Middle East, and Latin America.

Gavin covered every major financial network channel in the U.S. and internationally from Bloomberg, Bloomberg TV, Wall Street Journal, Reuters, Wharton's, Barron's, New York Times, and others for over two decades. He interviewed presidents, policy makers, fund managers, billionaire investors, and the wealthiest people in the world. He was also referenced at elite schools such as Harvard to Wharton's, and connected with financial institutions, EMPEA and International Monetary Fund (IMF). Further, he had successfully covered slum villages, communist and predominately Muslim countries, working with billionaire fund managers who have successfully generated good returns, while investing in frontier markets, and forecasting the next top 10 emerging markets poised to generate a good return on investment. The experiences he shared ranged from investments with fund managers in Wells Fargo to the slums of Vietnam.

In his quest for information that could lead to international headlines, and which separated investment from corruption, police brutality, and wars through communist and diplomatic democracies; he met Vincent Coyle, an Irish campaigner and Irish Bloody Sunday survivor. Vincent Coyle travels to remote places around the world raising awareness and promoting reconciliation among people and communities facing racial and political injustices.

Prior to my involvement within the financial sector, I was a writer, an ex-convict, a black man, and a father who had no control or leverage over my own life, or the future. I could not protect nor provide for the future generation, a generation I watched daily being eliminated politically, economically and socially through the media. Success seemed to be possible only for a few actors, athletes, and two-faced politicians. I represented a generation that was an asset during slavery and one that though contributing taxes, was excluded from voting, development and investment opportunities, and without control over the future.

Since the inception of President Donald Trump's '*Make America Great Again*' campaign, black people who had not achieved some level of success would be left behind. The working class could forget success except for the opportunities resurfacing through immigration reform, as there seemed to be a political and civil war on every front. It wasn't long before the Manafort trial started and every American was paying attention to each step of Special Counsel Robert Muller's potential indictment of President Trump or his son Donald Trump Jr., for conspiring with Russia, a foreign entity who had damaging information on the Democratic Nominee Hillary Clinton influencing the Presidential election. To add fuel to the fire, blacks were largely associated with the Democratic Party, and with every missed indictment that should have been given to then President Obama and nominee Hillary Clinton. This ultimately affected every black man who was encouraged by America's moving forward campaign, the successful election of the first black president, and alleged conspiracy crimes during Obama's two term presidency.

As a black author who had experienced the prejudices of economic discrimination, racial injustices, and police brutality; I was out actively facilitating knowledge on justice as a means to prevent youth from turning to crime. This was amidst the lack of civility after a video recording of unarmed black men being killed by the police resurfaced.

While Gavin's book unearthed a nearly transparent investment opportunity for both investors and policy makers, he had not expected that someone like me would be an avid reader of his book and a follower of his work. I was in over my head and a long haul, into solving the urban community's lack of ability to attract investment over and beyond law enforcement grants, jails, and prisons.

Trump touts that the Justice Department was not politically and publicly aligned with his past view of vindictive and selected prosecution, in the plight of urban New York City teens. Today the black community is under an undue amount of oppressive prosecution through the justice department, as Trump focuses on kneeling black athletes as not patriotic towards Americans' ideal captured in the patriotic anthem. Other than the fact that the Trump administration could be publicly associated with having committed some unknown political crimes, it was certain that the indictments, trials, convictions and guilty pleas in his administration had the same and/or similar problems the urban communities had been fighting which were as old as slavery. Additionally, the fact that the urban community made up less than average in political and economic leverage, posed a bigger challenge since everyone seemed to be emotionally and politically engaged in the transfer of power in the U.S.

Far from a Republicans and Democrats matter; it was now the affluent, poor whites and Republicans, against sympathetic whites and black Democrats, as Trump aligned with the Republicans.

Besides the fact that Gavin and Vincent had their history rooted deep into current world affairs interacting with political and business corruption, and dealt with investments that involved presidents, high officials, and lobbying organizations; Vincent had also dealt with government political and economic corruption, which prompted people to fight tooth and nail for the very rights the government was suppressing and especially democratic ideals. I on the other hand, was occupied with the real world and the world of democracy, freedom, and economic opportunity. Any word or stance from me, made it worse since it was like a slave protesting his own working wages.

There was fear behind America's criminalization of black males and the urban community that could only be changed by totally disengaging from the system. The black urban community was also unaware of the fact that they could attract investments. I would quote the Bible "man cannot live by bread alone" and was going to tell everyone that I knew about Vincent Coyle's work, invoke reconciliation and commit to selling thousands of books by Gavin Serkin. All this to prove there was interest in investing in the urban community, and for the urban community to understand the economic value.

This posed the real distance between the two extremes. One is the fact that no one knew or cared who I was in their circle of influence, and my circle of influence wasn't interested in what I was, who I was, nor who I cared to become. Later this worked to my benefit because it gave me ample time and opportunity to make a lot of mistakes and make a fool of myself, knocking on political and fund manager's doors trying to get support. It was mainly in the south the year earlier that reconciliation campaigner Vincent Coyle had come to support my cause. Alongside him, he brought Gavin the Head of Bloomberg's International Desk of Emerging Markets, I had not only read all of his books but studied all his published work. The fact that Tom Keene, the face of Bloomberg called Gavin the Rock Star of Finance, was enough to warrant my investigation and steadfastness.

The other fact I knew from studying the financial markets was that most institutional investors largely invest in the frontier markets, which come from the financial data that Bloomberg publishes. Bloomberg's data comes from various sources of financial influence from the perspective areas. The fact that Gavin was a Head in the International

Desk of Emerging Markets, meant that he had access to information that investors wanted. Black males were of no interest to him, and he was of no interest to them.

This was typical in politics, finance, and economic involvement areas in the U.S., as well as in frontier markets where relationships are vital to the information. One looks at the relationship with financial data internationally (blacks and whites), and also at the make up in the U.S. which is predominately white. Besides, assessing the country's demographics, the impact and return of the investments makes the difference on rate of returns. For instance, the make up in frontier markets is predominately people of color, and the institutional investors can make and or control the entire capacity of the market. Give or take, in a developed country markets are more developed or privy to competition.

The fact that large institutional investors and fund managers invest in frontier markets for a bigger margin of return than in developed markets, posed a potential problem in attracting any investment, apart from grants gained from the paying tax base. Yet these same developments in frontier market investment posed an opportunity to go out and build a base that could highlight an equal opportunity in the urban community.

Instead of creating a distraction for Gavin and the frontier market investment, I wanted to add value to the frontier markets and Gavin's work by getting more people involved. The rate of return for this new interest would create a reciprocal value in my circle of influence. In other words, we could see a lot of ourselves in frontier market investing.

We could use that interest not only to attract investments by getting involved in frontier markets through our direct investment, but also create more investors. Creation of investors was possible for the urban communities because they were a part of the funds and institutions invested in these markets. Soon those that were not investing would get interested and get involved.

I learned a lot about myself in the struggles I had in America and the racial relations, segregation, criminal justice system, and police brutality. I learned about South Africa by reading Mandela's Long Walk to Freedom and knew that the walk to making emerging markets attractive in the U.S., would face similar challenges. The abolition of slavery and integration had created unlimited opportunities, but also a list of challenges in economic integration.

The fact that you were free to create but without the ability to get around economic discretionary discrimination, was a major challenge because of self-preservation. Self-preservation was the first rule of law, and we were four or five generations behind in every aspect of the economic system and administration in the U.S. White Americans predominately held the administration jobs, councils, and positions that create budgets, tax receipts, and oversee distribution of funds. With the rise of technology and ease of access, the distribution of wealth and opportunity has drastically changed, but not without the burden of getting prepared to create, challenge, and control opportunities to be economically integrated and stable.

The fact that I was on a panel of international thought leaders with Gavin and Vincent, has a history to it that I'll share later in this book. For now, an idea of the magnitude of Gavin's work is that he had written one of few books ever funded and published by Bloomberg.

Every day, trillions of dollars in investments is traded in the markets that Bloomberg reports. Political regimes and market makers are also made and wiped out overnight at this and equal rate.

Countries can virtually change with Bloomberg reporting which provides data on markets, laws and wars from sanctions or tariffs. Importantly, the financial journalists travel in places most people cannot, to provide economic data on the markets. Gavin's work has been referenced in association with reporting agencies that credit worthy bond rates of countries, and rating companies such as the BMI Index. It's noteworthy to say his research and words mean something to institutional investors who generate returns from these markets, as they look for population, innovation, and demographics that attract investments.

I took the liberty to state that these conditions for investments and returns can be met with a profit for investors in urban communities, who historically have not been invested in nor leveraged in a productive way. It is a long-standing opportunity for future generations that has been missed until now. The population and demographics are there and even with a large base involved with the criminal justice system, a byproduct of lack of development, can be leveraged in a better way.

First I had to discover who, how, and why. I thought of the possibilities if only I could attract high profile people like Vincent and Gavin to my platform. To achieve this, I had to either have an investment opportunity or America was in grave international trouble. Even more troubling was the fact that I had to compete against discrimination.

Taxes received are distributed through a budget and agenda that even a tax paying citizen in the urban community has no way of influencing, for investment, grant, or employment opportunities due to discrimination. Not to mention the fact that blacks are not recruited into the system, thus no chance of changing the cycles of funding and opportunity distribution. From Bloomberg Business, EMPEA Global Private Equity Conferences, YALE Club New York, to the United

Nations Headquarters in New York, I had not quite figured out how to portray urban communities as an attractive asset to institutional investors that take trillions of dollars in funds to emerging assets.

I was quickly learning how the urban communities as an emerging asset, could access local federal and state tax budgets. It wasn't long before I realized that urban communities in America could be marketed in order to attract institutional investment. This was achievable through targeting, building, and harnessing the population's raw labor force and talents to develop and modernize their infrastructure. The move would also aid in assisting developing countries through their resources, to create opportunities.

AITFM-AMERICAN INSTITUTE OF TRADING THE FINANCIAL MARKETS

AITFM

A ITFM was supposed to solve issues, and it all started with a group of nine inmates who were incarcerated for various crimes ranging from drug conspiracy, fraud, and embezzlement and more. The goal was to forecast the trades of the financial markets and get the information to someone on the outside to place the trades. First the market had to be understood, and that required that the inmates use their limited resources to learn the different aspects of the market. An inmate nicknamed Dow Jones facilitated the idea since he was a successful real-estate salesman, entrepreneur, and investor.

Unlike Trump he was the subject of a real witch hunt that was easily a conviction. Yet, the head of the intelligence division, justice department, amongst others were on the international news as untrustworthy institutions. It is a distrust that was attached to their leadership and handling of investigations, which crippled defendant's lives before the facts were established. Just like events have been happening under the watch of the ousted leadership of President Trump, people around the world have seen the effects the justice department has had on urban communities. Now we are at a crossroads where those investigations are implied upon the cabinet and person of the Office of President of the United States.

Surprisingly in prison Dow Jones had a shorter sentence and more resources and was able to access books, magazine subscriptions, and even more importantly, the cellphones used to communicate the trades.

The group of nine had an assignment to read books on the stock market supplied from outside the prison. The books were well over 500 pages and contained new information for each of us. Some of us had been incarcerated since the late 1980s and early 1990s when inmates who could afford it, joined forces with convicted industry professionals who would trade stocks, bonds, and commodities running to millions in margin accounts. Some of them had the money and were traders and brokers before incarceration. The Bureau of Prisons put a limit on business and transactions that an inmate could do and phone restrictions of 300 minutes a month which made it very hard to trade but increased the need for cellphones.

There were also professionals from other backgrounds who would hold classes to assist inmates to learn about their fields and pass the time. Everyone thought they could or needed to learn business since it was the only option alongside fears of getting back in good graces without an education or opportunity.

I had been incarcerated about nine years at this point and had taken every business class I could. I was hoping Don King's quote about reading enough books on business could help. Not to mention Les Brown's recommendation that if you read 60 books on any particular title, you could be part of the upper echelon of the professionals in that field in terms of knowledge. I needed all this advice and a bit of luck. I'd had my share of trouble learning but with all the time I had served and had left to do, I could learn some more. To my advantage, most times I was a loner and felt that most inmates were too involved in nonsense, and less involved in constructive learning and that alone kept me engrossed. One example is that there was only one typewriter for every 1000 inmates, and it was in the law library.

I knew the agreement among us was that after successful trading we would each net 10k. I made a decision on the subject I would pursue, and I knew the rest would not be interested. It was a motivation driven by the thought that I could end up with all the money if I learned every subject. I worked hard and found that all the books were right up my alley. I had the opportunity to learn all the material in books that cost up to $100.00 each, which was priceless in prison.

I had a gut feeling that the group would not last long enough, and I was proven right when members of the group took advantage of what they had learned and formed their own groups. I had written several books by this time e.g. one on real estate investment – a manuscript I lost. With the reality of this pre-empted disbursement of the group I redirected my efforts to financial markets. I ended up being a key member in the group and eventually one of the founders of AITFM - American Institute of Trading the Financial Markets.

The first step was to set up trades and we ended up getting busted for breaking every rule in the system. Dow Jones ended up in disciplinary segregation as the mastermind of our system. We learned so much about money through the studies that we knew how to follow the trail of money. It wasn't until we started charting the Wall Street Journal and paper trading that we met an ex-banker who told us that all the Wall Street data indicated where money goes. As an experienced professional he helped us to create the instruments of trade through stock exchanges and funding companies using private placement memorandums.

I was learning a lot and it wasn't long before I was studying the market 24/7. As I read all financial related articles I noticed that the effects on forecasting world events, followed the release of economic data around the world. It was not an easy task studying the financial markets with no formal education.

Besides, the fact that the market was too big for manipulation and the hyped-up stories like the Wolf of Wall Street, Jordan Belfort, and eventually Madoff, there was no better place I desired to spend my time. It felt like I was learning my way out of poverty and was close to finding the secret behind the success of professionals making a living from trading the markets. The most interesting aspect though was making money educating others about how the market operates.

AITFM connected people who had no control over their finances and financial security by providing information on trading. In any case larger institutional investors were also trading financial markets through these exchanges.

It wasn't long before we gained enough interest to join market learning sessions that went on all day and night. I would study all day and report findings to the group at night. It was a commitment that required staying up late at night and being the first to turn on news in the morning considering that there were no market channels. We soon learned that not only did news follow world events, but the market also predicted the events. Further, we found out that prison related instruments were also traded on the stock exchanges. It was heart wrenching to know that our freedom was directly related to the field of study that could change our fortunes. Notwithstanding, the lessons were a good way to initiate constructive conversations.

After several months of charting the market with the group, we conducted our first trade successfully. Our founder Dow Jones was released, and this moved the group from books to connecting with established companies, institutions, investment funds, and philanthropists. This was an avenue to solving social problems within our community and returning to society.

AITFM also educated the community on how to trade the financial markets using technical analysis, considering that over four trillion dollars a day flow through the market. It was a huge market and impossible to manipulate but beneficial when understood. Founded by a couple of guys who had nothing but time on their hands, the group included stockbrokers, stock traders, market makers, and more added to the portfolio. Initially we started with paper trading using the Wall Street Journal and world news, and later were able to forecast the rise of gold using the investor yield curve in the early 2000s.

I also successfully predicted the success of Sirius and XM Satellite radio since its inception, after learning about it from Private Placement memorandums, National Investors Network of Angel Investors with Karen Rand a burgeoning author, podcast and TV personality in Atlanta, Georgia to Mike Segal host of one of the largest East Coast Private Equity Conferences held annually in New York. We were part of a group that not only exchanged money but knew where money could be solicited from Hedge Fund Managers, Angel and Venture Capitalist Fund managers, Retired CEO's and corporate executives with a wealth of retirement.

AITFM started with the study of technical analysis, charting the Wall Street Journal from cover to cover, and day trading demos. This was because we had no idea that these weren't the real indicators. We read John Murphy's Global Technical Analysis books that taught us how the overall markets are connected, and the greatest lesson was that all or most of the information showed where the money went. Private placements on the other hand, indicated where money was going. We found out also that it was important to know what IPOs meant.

One of my favorite movies to date is Social Network about the founding of Facebook. Even more apparent was the level of wealth in Greenwich, Connecticut and more in the private equity field from hedge funds and more. Movies like The Wolf of Wall Street and more displayed people who accumulated wealth and served less time than a bad check writer. Times had changed more since Enron and more so with corporate fraud, but nothing compared to the streets.

AITFM had all of the information that to date shows where and why institutional investors trade and invest. Again with the right product, private placement funding could get you listed on an exchange and eventually funded along with the right exit strategy to avoid the risk factors that expose small companies.

I watched 50 cent and Master P on BET in the Basement, when Master P told 50 cent there were just a few 100 million-dollar men in the black community, but in private equity they were under 25 making 100 to 200 million a year and had 20 to 25 car garages. I had just read about the wealth of these investors and managers in Stocks and Commodities Magazine.

Further, the fact that the SEC created an exemption for fundraising with Private Placement Memorandums (PPM), allowed small companies to raise money by their shares to qualified investors, and signing risk disclosure documents bode well for the market. Knowledge and access to this market faced high levels of discretionary discrimination. Luckily there were a few diverse fund companies.

By this time, I was well connected to a group of young and middle age burgeoning capitalist minds, including professionals with backgrounds from Black Rock, Merrill Lynch, Bloomberg, Wells Fargo, and a host of Angel Networks, Ventures, and Private Equity professionals. We were making significant progress in attracting direct investment into the urban communities to be hedged along with investments in emerging markets. This would build stability in homes and get people to also build stability abroad.

Since all markets are connected, it is not only good for capital returns but also good to attract U.S. participation. Observing the status quo, and lack of diversity almost stopped us from engaging, but it seemed worse not to try to make forward progress.

Getting institutional investors to facilitate funding of social programs targeted at tackling social ills was taking root all over the world, e.g. Stockton California and the United Nations sustainable development goals were a focus within the EMPEA. It became apparent that financing was the vehicle that would move the populace towards economic prosperity, when I got involved in emerging and frontier markets. Money and investment have a lot to do with people's moral aptitude and solving problems by creating an appetite for success.

This book is the prelude to the institutional investments in the urban community, which will help reduce crime, poverty and the amount of tax money that funds the justice system, adding resources that build a community and homes, strengthening families. Noteworthy is that the same market that makes a criminal justice system is the same that can prevent crimes that cripple the community.

While the broke life of one person can cripple the family and community, it also justifies an industry that pays the employee who works in the system and could very well be a counselor in the school, or a security guard in the school. Through this, taxpayers will get better returns on their investment.

One problem is that fear promotes the need to beef up security, which in turn produces more violent interactions, and crimes that the system could never address. It's called discretionary discrimination, which can't be charged as a crime but produces crime because taxes paid by taxpayers never return any progress.

Secondly, it reduces trust between the administration and the community. The urban community needs an investment that will produce a return besides victimization by the criminal justice system which is a catalyst to crime and an ongoing lack of trust.

The era of corporate social responsability has forced so many companies into corrections, including Starbucks, Papa Johns, and more. It's an era where activist groups are going for impact investing. The truth of the matter is that if integrated cooperative economic inclusion was going to reach the level of institutional investment coupled with community collective cooperation at the city and county level, it was going to be a straight black effort without the support of the U.S. system that had systematically enslaved the community.

I had come from a horrendous experience of drugs, prison, streets, and experienced the criminal justice system through arrest, bond, pre-trial, lawyers, and house arrest. However, I had no idea about the effort it took trying to upright a sunken ship.

I believed that people in high places had an intention of enabling and helping improve the country for those doing the right thing, in addition to preventing them from doing the wrong thing. Well this was not the case because people in high places simply did only what they could as part of doing right. The justice system was a byproduct of those doing right against the wrongdoers and not what I had assumed. It was not a case of good people helping others to stay away from the wrong choices, or even understanding their choices or how to prevent making these choices. Inarguably the criminal justice system had a life of its own, and if you were down you were down, with only luck as your way of getting help.

The other fact is that; it was becoming obvious that the criminal justice system was a wild animal. A wild animal that we all had and have to deal with at some point in our lives if black and male.

First it was a wave of attacks with the Enron probe and then Russia, then the meth and opioid problem could be singled out to whites. However, the fact that no police were convicted of a crime displayed a flaw in the system. Nevertheless, the issue remains that Manafort could be charged in a 70-million-dollar case and hundreds of transactions, and only two people would be indicted.

This relates to Trump as well because when I first went into prison, I remember reading an article that stated that the founders of the constitution had no idea that prosecutors would have free reign over their work, and no one could police them. They could legally commit crimes against humanity, and no one could prove the burden. Later I learned about Harmless Error, which if I had known about earlier might have led to a different outcome during my trial. In other words, there is a lot of discrimination and corruption built into every facet of society, and when you are going against the system, nothing will prevent the wheels from turning. The unfavorable nature of the system is because it is heavily funded and relied upon in making sure that no one will go against it. This means that we have to invest in deterrence and divest it to other measures of our society.

Focusing on school and education is one approach, but I am into direct community investment. Just as you would invest in a business to be successful, communities also need investors and having the best of choices is fundamental.

If the entire urban community has to rely on change, then their position is based on voting and tax base. With access to world markets, investment, and marketing tools with technology improving lives can happen rather quickly.

In order for the tax system to survive and balance tax receipts and budget, there must be investment in the community. If you go to the markets that serve jobs in our community, there is a demand for the highest level of education in technical and skilled jobs, and schools offering training and education are readily available. However, closely studying the community one does not see a community that wants to take advantage of these opportunities.

A change in this attitude starts at the community level even if America has a bias in every aspect on matters involving blacks. It is a bias observed in ownership of property, business, and investment to politics, humanity and other related aspects. In order to capitalize on this, companies must attract investment and jobs to increase productivity. Also they must attract people to move closer to reduce drive time, energy expenditure, and responding to employees' concerns on convenience.

Since one cannot merely attract talent and people to buy homes and build a base, investment coupled with impact investing and activism will provide the energy where it is needed. Therefore, there is a need for more technical schools with partnered business programs that lead to internships with pay and competition. This will ultimately lead to increased labor for the industries.

EXAMPLES OF SUCCESSFUL PROGRAMS

Programs for students such as job shadowing in companies within the community give them an opportunity to select three career options under guidance of professionals in the field. However, personal challenges in the students' lives overwhelm their thinking. This is besides the perception that it's hard to succeed on their own without any investment interest. Good grades, and good intentions are not good enough but its carefully planned collaboration can help make all the difference.

Investment Money Required in These Communities include:

1. Money to pair single mothers with case managers (transportation, insurance, medical)

2. Money to provide low-income families with a "word pedometer" and biweekly coaching from trained home visitors

3. Money for mental-health clinicians (hygiene, healthcare, clothing, speech, eyes, dental etc...)

4. Money for anti-violence counselors

5. Money for college coaches

6. Money for green spaces and sustainable-food hubs

7. Money to support psychotherapy centers

Other areas that require investment (financial and time) are: college post-graduation plans, local business apprenticeships, career fairs, guided job search programs, resume writing, interviews, social media networking, etiquette classes, interview dress, and job shadowing and volunteering opportunities.

PUBLIC EDUCATION AND MENTAL HEALTH

Before our children even set foot into public or private schools to compete for an education that leads to a career, there is an aspect of mental health.

Thousands of programs are introduced through 501©(3), to address mental health, and social services amongst other issues in urban communities. These are issues affecting our children, and eventually keep them out of pursuing a career.

As the biggest challenge facing people in the world is making a decent wage to facilitate a decent living, businesses and communities also have to make enough returns to pay their employees and this translates to increased productivity.

When a child is five years old, he must see the community's hand in his development. The jobs in the community must also serve his development, and the financial service sectors facilitate his access to credit, loans, taxes, and lending for leverage over the productivity of his earnings.

Altogether, as the philanthropists are told, the opportunities to invest totals millions of dollars per city and billions per state. In the next 20 years every urban area can be a model city for emerging communities, and urban transformation given endorsement by mayors and city managers. It is such an investment that can eradicate the housing crisis and help produce:

1. Income

2. Local community organizations

Private investments and donors are also key to this development so that the city doesn't have to raise taxes. This is still only one half of what is needed because the government ultimately collects taxes. Therefore, a grant could be possible given the community tax base or potential tax base. Besides, it solves problems people cannot solve.

To date people cannot operate at a benevolent rate because they are challenged economically, socially, and emotionally. This begs the question on how planting a seed is not sustainable? The answer is simple; they don't want it to grow since it is competition against their laziness.

3 BONDS-INVESTMENT-RETURNS

A municipal bond is issued by a local government generally to finance public projects such as: roads, schools, airports, repairs among other functions.

Municipal bonds may be general obligations of the issuer or secured by specified revenues and in the United States, interest income received by holders of municipal bonds is often excluded from gross income for federal income tax purposes.

TYPES OF MUNICIPAL BONDS

General Obligation and Revenue Bonds

Municipal bonds provide tax exemption from federal taxes and many state and local taxes, depending on the laws of each state. Municipal securities consist of both short-term issues (often called notes, which typically mature in one year or less) and long-term issues (commonly known as bonds, which mature in more than one year).

Short-term notes are used by an issuer to raise money for a variety of reasons such as, anticipation of future revenues such as taxes, state or federal aid payments; future bond issuances; covering irregular cash flows; meeting unanticipated deficits; and raising immediate capital for projects until long-term financing can be arranged. Bonds are usually sold to finance capital projects over the longer term.

The Two Basic Types of Municipal Bonds Are:

General obligation bonds: Principal and interest are secured by the full faith and credit of the issuer and usually supported by either the issuer's unlimited or limited taxing power. In many cases, general obligation bonds are voter approved.

Revenue bonds: Principal and interest are secured by revenues derived from tolls, charges or rents from the facility, built with the proceeds of the bond issue. Public projects financed by revenue bonds include toll roads, bridges, airports, water and sewage treatment facilities, hospitals and subsidized housing. Many of these bonds are issued by special authorities created for that particular purpose.

INSTITUTION INVESTMENTS

An institutional investor is an entity which pools money to purchase securities, real property, and other investment assets or originate loans.

Institutional investors include banks, insurance companies, pensions, hedge funds, REITs, investment advisors, endowments, and mutual funds. Operating companies which invest excess capital in these types of assets may also be included in the term.

Activist institutional investors may influence corporate governance by exercising voting rights in their investments.

PRIVATE EQUITY

Private equity typically refers to investment funds organized as limited partnerships that are not publicly traded and whose investors are typically large institutional investors, university endowments, or wealthy individuals.

Private equity firms are known for their extensive use of debt financing to purchase companies, which they restructure and attempt to resell for a higher value.

Debt financing reduces corporate taxation burdens and is one of the principal ways in which private equity firms make business more profitable for investors.

HOUSING AND BASIC INCOME

HOUSING CDC BLOCK GRANTS CRA-COMMUNITY REINVESTMENT ACT -BANKING AND FINANCE

BANKING AND FINANCE- CRA penalize every bank that does not give back to the community it borrows from. For instance, Bank of America/Merrill Lynch in South Carolina deposits 12 billion lends mortgages worth 300 million and grants 1.5 million.

LONDON ENGLAND MARK MOBIUS

London is hours ahead of U.S. Eastern standard time, but Gavin Serkin had tagged me in on a tweet with Mark Mobius during their travels. Mark Mobius, who is regarded as a pioneer and Godfather of Emerging Market Investment, worked together with Gavin on his book on Frontier where he wrote the epilogue.

I had been working very hard to create awareness among people on Emerging Market investing, and the benefits achieved by investors and the communities where there was investment. However, my focus was on how I could attract investors from our community and activate interest in investment and educate the people. The more people that got involved the more peace and prosperity would exist in the community.

Gavin took note of my interest, recorded his surprise in my interest and even stated that Frontier was not ideally written with readers like me in mind. Frontier in its position targeted investors with the intention of helping them make great returns off the grid markets. I informed my support team that we would soon be studied by billionaires within a span of two years later.

Gavin continued working closely with Mark Mobius and they bought a company in Myanmar called Vinamilk. It is a business move that raised close to a billion dollars. Gavin would later interview Mark Mobius after Brexit news, where Mark Mobius mentioned that the asset acquisition was facilitated by innovation, cellphones and social media revolution. The same was observed in the financial inclusion strategies for Safaricom. Gavin and I knew this was bound to happen for every community including urban communities in the U.S.

It took me nearly three years to establish how Gavin's book could help the local communities, and this was through institutional investors.

Institutional investors would invest in our communities just like in international communities. Further research led to the mayor later confirming that we needed to get started in the building of these required connections.

BUSINESS DEVELOPMENT ALLIANCES

At this point I had met with the local Mayor, who was a huge fan of the work we were seeking to do around the city by connecting the urban community to local government, politics, business, social, and civic engagement. Our interest was to help the people learn how things worked around them, e.g. the Mayor oversees developments within the city and monitors concerns before they fester. We had not yet met with the city planner, although he had made an inquiry about our efforts. As the city recorded a surge in gangs and drug related activities, with some residents being part of high-profile shootings and murder, complaints were soaring. City leaders had been meeting regularly to find ways to engage the community and curb further violence in the area, but when they slowed down more shootings and violence would occur.

The youthful population was very active on social media and related arenas but not engaged in the community socially. It was a long-term project trying to get people to be active in parts of the city that recorded an upsurge of crime. However, the effort was worthwhile in preventing further decline in social and civic engagement.

We actively sought to generate sponsorship in areas where the youth were more interested in sports and entertainment than civic and social engagement. The plan under deliberation was long-term and would bring major corporations and donors to directly invest in the area. It seemingly was the only idea besides raising taxes in order to meet the needs of the community.

The approach was going to be threefold; i. Community leaders to fully participate in the developments, ii. Local industries to directly donate, and sponsors and organizations in the area to help them generate income to heighten their profiles, and iii. City leaders to reach out to institutions serving residents and invite all organizations around the city offering mental health support and related concerns.

The Chamber of Commerce directly aided in establishment, overseeing aspects of marketing and connecting of the businesses in increasing exposure. It was necessary since businesses in the urban community rarely established themselves with corporate groups within the Chamber of Commerce, besides consuming a few of their services. The most significant activity was to increase our exposure.

The local Small Business Development Association (SBDA) were being sponsored by the State Economic Department, and it helped in building, guiding, and directing these businesses and entrepreneurs to available resources within their industry.

We worked with this team in facilitating the needs of the urban community, a community that was not aware of resources available for the SBDA. Some of these resources were in retrospect free services and included; business plan development, social media and website development amongst others. The local vocational center director worked between school students, industries, and business needs, teaching and developing students' vocational and technical skills. This would satisfy the needed workforce demand within the local and surrounding communities. All were on hand and helped coordinate required public service works and providing resources to the community, and work credit to the students.

We had associated ourselves with business leaders who we could collaborate with on current and future business opportunities. The workforce development organization was also interested in partnering with us to help in sharpening the students' skills and readiness for job interviews and the professional world. The need for preparedness for the professional world was observed when the youth turned up for interviews wearing slippers, cellphones in their hands, and wearing inappropriate clothing for the job. Some even lacked soft skills needed to land a job and needed to learn proper business etiquette such as firm handshakes.

During the introduction of Samsung, the #1 brand for home appliances in North America, they committed over 300 million in an investment facility that Caterpillar had abandoned. Prior to closure of the facility, I had made a presentation on Caterpillar at a Bloomberg session drawing points from their journey and making a comparison with other companies overseas.

The closure of Caterpillar was the subject of discussion in the Business Alliance meeting, amidst community uproar as hundreds lost their source of livelihood. 20 miles up the road there was a further loss of 5000 jobs, on abandonment of an expansion project for the nuclear power plant.

We had to ponder over some key issues such as were manufacturers responding to the entry of Samsung into the community, were they interested in the opportunity for their cost benefits, was there a need for a festival to introduce these investors to the community and its culture, was it feasible to have jobs attracting labor ranging 40-50 miles outside the county, what plans were necessary for hiring etc. I envisioned diversity but 30% of the population in the community was unemployed.

Notwithstanding the concerns, there was an opportunity for the community to pitch itself within the direct line of institutional investment. The Work Force Development Organization was a good platform to recruit workers, but the talent required further development and this meant direct sponsorship would have to be a prelude to the Work Force Development.

Besides Work Force Development, organizations and administrations attracting these institutions were funded by taxes and contractors were hired. This meant that the urban community would not even receive 1% of these payments, thus nothing would stream back into the community, nor would there be jobs. It meant developing capacity to handle technical inquiries and improve business competition.

2 POLITICS-POLICY-ACTIVISM

Politics is the way that groups make decisions. It is about agreements between people enabling peaceful co-existence among tribes, cities, or countries. Depending on the size of the group, more time might be required for developing these agreements. It is important to note that the people who are central to politics are referred to as politicians. Politicians and other people may get together to form a government, with subsequent academic studies on politics in universities classified under political science, political studies, or public administration.

In our everyday affairs the term "politics" refers to the way that countries are governed, and how governments make rules and laws. Politics can also be observed in other groups besides government, such as in companies, clubs, schools, and churches.

Governments

The government makes an effort to lead an entire group within its jurisdiction through activities such as;

- Deciding land allocation

- Deciding those who are in charge

- Deciding on security matters etc.

Create money

Build things for collective use such as roads, hospitals, libraries, and docks

Educate people, either for their own good, or to understand what the government wants them to know

Take care of the very young, the sick, or the very old

Manage the welfare of the country and manage the money available for spending on services (Hospitals, Schools, etc.)

One of the ways the government leads the group is by making laws and rules which tell everybody what they can and cannot do. The government makes these laws so that the society is safe and orderly. For example, the law that prohibits driving while under the influence of alcohol, stops people from drunk driving. The law that you must wear a helmet while riding a motorcycle, ensures that a person protects themselves.

The government also controls people and events that take place in a country through other means besides making laws. For example, government spending makes a big difference in people's choices and actions. If the government spends more on hospitals people will probably become healthier. Also, if people perceive their government as wise and positively respond to the government they are highly likely to obey this particular government.

Politics is often compared to ethics (an abstract study of right and wrong). Ethics is more concerned with principles than law, politics or diplomacy, and this leads to many thinking it's not practical. However, without some agreement on ethics, there is probably no way to even have a debate, laws, or an election. Notwithstanding, there is always some agreement on ethics and personal conduct in a political system.

Political parties

In most countries, people have formed political parties to propel forward their ideas. Despite disagreements between party members, they always find a way to work together considering that they have more to agree upon and join forces than disagree. Party members can agree to take the same position on many issues, support changes to laws amongst other things. It is however important to note that elections are key for political parties and are characterized by competition between the different parties.

International politics

Disagreements also exist between different countries and attempts to bring solutions through meetings is referred to as diplomacy. Diplomacy is basically politics between nations, and if issues are not resolved through the diplomatic meetings this can lead to war or terrorism.

4 FINANCE –LOANS-RETURNS

Commercial Banking

A commercial bank is an institution that provides services such as accepting deposits, providing business loans, and offering basic investment products. Commercial banks can also refer to a bank, or a division of a large bank, which more specifically deals with deposit and loan services that are provided to corporations or large/ middle-sized business - as opposed to individual members of the public/small business.

Besides hustling and being entrepreneurial, few people really know how to build a successful business credit profile to secure commercial loans, position for more funding and stay competitive within the market. These credit profiles include Dun and Bradstreet numbers, tax id, business bank account, incorporation, web sites, and landline phone services.

Paying taxes is essential to leveraging on lending since it shows ones bottom-line ability to pay off loans, just like net income from employment allows one to borrow with credit.

Banking

A bank is a financial institution that accepts deposits from the public and creates credit.

Most people and especially those living in the urban community have little insight into the structure of how finance and banking works. This is a phenomenon arising from the fact that they were born to hard-working families, with local businesses and credit with local financing forms. The arrangement with these local community financiers was that one can finance their food and necessities by borrowing and making payments at pay day. We were in no way bank customers but ultimately, were financed from the economy we had built with the loan interests. Then came credit with the banks and we had only local credit and financing that was not reported to the financial institutions, today it would be buy here pay here.

Today even prepay, buy here and pay here, and rent companies are getting in the credit reporting business as a way to attract customers who are now getting more informed with the increased accessibility and usage of the internet. There is another component to banking that's the difference between banks and credit unions. Credit Unions are usually easier to create a relationship with, since you can join as a member. Banks may require a higher credit score in comparison to Credit Unions.

Another financial issue facing urban communities is credit. While most noncredit related bills take up a large portion of income, it does not help build credit like cellphone bills, rent and medical bills. In some cases, e.g. late payment of student loans ruins an individual's credit score for decades and more. Everything from buying a car, house and even furniture comes with double digit interest rates.

This credit issue is usually passed down through generations because of the repairs to the cars, the inability to buy a home, and paying rent that never helps increase the purchasing options. For example, you purchase a car with higher payment and miles. This car will require constant repairs that you have to take out a loan to fix. During this time, you will have to seek other avenues to facilitate your movement e.g. getting a taxi to take you to and from work. The next possible situation is that the car which is in repo is reported to the credit bureau, demanding that you go to a buy here pay here to recover from the earlier situation. It is this cycle and downward spiral that continues affecting your job, health, psychology etc.

I advocate for total debt forgiveness through new reporting standards that will let a person take classes and become affiliated with companies' growth.

INVESTMENT AND FINANCE

If you invest in insurance companies who also finance investments, you can literally take a portion of your returns for retirement. They invest your money and pay you a return that eventually you add to your retirement depending on your contribution amount.

The urban community pays taxes but rarely invests for retirement except social security. A lot of health issues usually lead to early disability and if you are fortunate to have a good job, you may have a life or whole life insurance policy with some cash value to leave behind for your family upon death. There are tons of financial advisers who sell these products in the urban community e.g. Primerica and a host of others now on the internet who sell services to urban consumers. However, the lack of sufficient income is a major hindrance to improvement of an individual's quality of life through these services which require investing.

Financial planners can take you through an array of options to help you mobilize your life, maximize your income, and help preserve your estate. They sell annuities from your investments and can help you create the passive income you need to ward off late in life financial problems. Also, they help you arrange for possible issues and occurrences such as sickness, death, and disability.

Retirement plans are huge investment opportunities and if you are not the recipient of one, it's a good start to put one in place for your next generation so that they have better opportunities. Retirement 401K plans match your contributions over the course of the agreements and options such as 529 College Plans assist in funding education. These funds can often be monitored as mentioned in the earlier chapter on frontier and emerging markets.

5 REAL ESTATE-PROPERTY-LEVERAGE

In Newberry, South Carolina, the city has a budget of 75 million for a population of 38k and property taxes account for 76% of the revenue. A portion of the city's income comes from venue fees, events, parades, and more. The administration divides the budget by departments as approved by city and country councils where contracts and contractors are paid to fulfill the agendas set forth by the same.

The urban community has no representation other than labor to fulfill the low-end jobs, since they are not qualified based on school or technical training to fulfill requirements of higher paying jobs. The people who hold the high-level government jobs as well as contractors, commute back and forth from nearby counties. The challenge the local community faced was in growth and retaining home grown talent who were attracted to high-end jobs in other communities. Therefore, the gap between attracting and keeping the talent kept getting harder as companies offered more perks. Usually it's a wise investment to have an industry that brings a market and suppliers to help the local community grow.

Gavin sat on a panel with Vincent Coyle at Newberry College where he compared his work with billionaires and individuals, his work was founded to help produce economic empowerment for individuals working in their community. I had recently been working with the college on a community college connection to produce my film on Justice System Awareness. The City Police, College President, Mayor, and local news outlet all agreed it could be a success although we had not finalized a budget for production.

There had been aggressive support for our efforts and even reconciliation after the shooting at Mother Emanuel Church, which prompted a call for our work in the community. It wasn't long before we were invited to be a part of Dufford Diversity Week honoring Bill Dufford, a white man who had become a local pioneer in diversity integration in the school system. Dufford was also a big contributor to Newberry College's diversity program. At a church where he grew up, a black veteran was denied entrance to a worship service and was forced to travel some miles away to congregate with fellow blacks.

The panel was a success until we went for dinner and were later faced by the hostile reality that no big shots were to be in town with the little folks. It is this sentiment that led to my being branded racist and not promoting justice inform, reconciliation, and economic inclusion. Our supporters included Bloomberg, United Nations Reconciliation campaigner Vincent Coyle, and Billy Graham Evangelistic Association whose ministry had expanded over five decades. They stood with us at the State Capitol grounds and this finally opened a door.

DISCRETIONARY DISCRIMINATION

Blacks do not own and or control most of the noted wealth in land, resources, businesses, etc. in any city or state in America. It is also worth noting that they neither occupy many of the jobs in administrations and businesses that collect or distribute taxes, or draft policies and processes facilitating wealth creation.

Governments are also observed to distribute taxes to competing businesses, that rarely end up in the hands of urban communities. It is the development of such businesses, supported by policies that also attract industries, plants, and manufacturers that presents an opportunity for job creation and community development.

Initially the underdeveloped communities invest in their own industries which are usually not taxed, funded, nor well structured to leverage on available funding. This condition maintains the status quo even as the available talent remains dormant or unutilized.

While in their initial state we observe an opportunity in the reinvestment with direct institutional investment playing a key role. The institutions sponsorship connects, develops, and drives talent, increasing productivity in the marketplace and creating a wider tax base as taxpayers' increase. The end result is a reduction in costs arising from crime, driving up markets and consumption.

When I started to learn financial literacy, I was bitter since I thought slavery had gotten my family off to a winless start, followed by a limited pool of choices in the post slavery era. See I was born in the South in the early seventies and what this meant was that I was only a generation down from the cotton fields, and slightly away from the straight plantations and slave ships. So yes I was bitter. However, there was an aspect of my own guilt arising from the knowledge that while I grew up working in the fields and cotton mills, I had lost the drive for hard work. I had been enticed into the world of entertainment and spending more time in bars and clubs.

People worked hard all week, but they also partied just as hard over the weekends. Everything seemed hard until the weekend when I got myself into trouble and discovered that my poor choices over the weekends made weekdays even harder. It was a trail of trouble as I was either fixing a car that was wrecked from drunk driving, paying back bond money because of a DUI charge, or finding myself in a fist and knife fight. In all this drama, blacks and whites didn't mingle unless they were well acquainted through work displaying a relationship that had no taint of racism.

Outside of all this a different story was projected, one of equality but in retrospect, it was that blacks and whites were happy with the separation. As usual the whites had done a number on the blacks, and even after slavery and segregation was gone economic disparity remained strong. It was all for the whites and none to the blacks, and then came integration and taxes and blacks needed jobs from the whites. When taxes were collected and administrations hired enough capacity to facilitate distribution, blacks were busy constructing industries for the whites as they proceeded for vacations.

The deal was done, and blacks went on to work in those industries, and did not secure the administration jobs because whites were deep into the fourth and fifth generations. Blacks tried voting but neither did that lead to election of officials who could gain them much traction. Looking back at the situation it was satisfactory on paper and according to the photos, but the economic and money trail did not match this outlook for the black community. The disparities led blacks to creation of their own hustles, entrepreneurship and industries after paying taxes and bills with the little money left for investment which had to be topped up with borrowing. It is a cycle that has maintained the same rhythm to date. Dr. King said that the Negro in America would either be *America's greatest asset or greatest liability*. Nevertheless, to this very day America has not re-invested in the black community, and most platforms that have received some form of subsidy from the government to mend the economic ills have only managed to cover a small percentage of the deep-seated issues.

Dr. King said that if America was to right its wrongs to the American Negro it would not have any money for seed. Therefore, my message to you is that you have to paint yourselves. I realized that unless we attracted direct investment by increasing our value, our vote (though a good part of the plan) was not going to be enough to pull us out the ghetto of America. We were going to have to clean up, clean up, and clean up some more, and that would have to start with our greatest institutions namely, healthcare, churches, homes and schools. Organizing ourselves on the political front was not going to progress the community either because with each set of hands and powers goes another subsidy rant, which rendered us needier and dependent, oblivious of the fact that we could change and control the situation by creating an interdependence relationship connecting all parties involved.

I couldn't stay mad because whites were going on doing their business. While some protested President Trump knowing full well they had not truly ushered in President Obama, others did not realize that a government could only go so far within the confines of laws, customs and policy.

I was now facing myself, and even with all the meetings I held behind closed doors, the truth is that not much could be done. It was important that one went out and brought something of value to facilitate the desired change. In this case, I had to deliver more fuel to the fire by inviting businesses and individuals who could partner up with the established institutions. The collective value was optimistically aimed at producing a return or I would have to create the opportunities.

The past and current administrations and systems held no sympathy. Therefore, business meetings had to start with churches buying municipal bonds backing the collateral in our communities and leveraging on loans whilst partnering with local government administrations. The partnerships were a conduit to some of the programs that offered government grant money that could help save money and solve a couple of the existing problems. The Mayor, City Managers, and administrations built 5, 10, 15, and 20 year campaigns meant to attract people back to the community, but they would not necessarily bear the brunt of fixing the ills marginalized people were still dealing with.

First of all, marginalized communities must address the discretionary discrimination where blacks could get a return on the taxes they pay, this would be a good start. Further, festivals, vendors and organizations working in the communities with proper funding, would become more productive remitting more taxes and ultimately adding value to the community and attracting additional investment.

FINANCIAL LITERACY

I was angry after I heard Counselor Cortez play Rich Dad Poor Dad and quote that the only thing more money taught every poor person without financial literacy, was that they didn't know what to do with it. Further he stated that what the rich knew about money, the poor and middle class did not. The rich people then taught their children what they knew about money and future generations of the poor and middle class again missed out on the information. He also added that it wasn't what the poor people knew or didn't know about money, rather as in his case, it was who they knew and what they had been taught about the difference between rich, poor and middle class. All this was a myth in my case, because while in prison most were there for money related crimes i.e. through robbery of fraud.

Away from the glass ceilings in their high-rise offices was a vivid written travelogue of billionaire investors and fund managers, while the story was different on the ground in slums in over 10 countries. These countries had the potential to lead economic growth, a fact confirmed in the immeasurable returns made and wealth accumulated in the U.S. while investing in off- the- grid emerging economies. It is an accumulation of wealth that was gained as they solved the social problems of those societies.

It was not going to be an easy task to connect extreme ends of the market together. Extremes broken since the abolition of slavery, when slaves became tax paying citizens. Either way I was willing to take chances, because of the threat of brute injustices and exclusion. Regardless of the disparity it was never too late to make an effort to remedy the woes.

There was an article about the young black 27-year-old City Mayor who hosted a funding tour, to get philanthropists and investors to buy up social programs that would help integrate the challenged community back into mainstream America. We'd been working for nearly a decade to enter the financial markets as an instrument to change our social ills. I was conscious that it would take unearthing of the political and economic structures for better understanding.

1 BUDGET-TAXES-CIRCULATORY DISCRIMINATION

Budgets are political instruments that weigh policy priorities against available public resources; specify the ways and means of providing public programs and services; establish the cost of programs and the criteria by which these programs will be evaluated for efficiency and effectiveness; ensure that the programs will be evaluated at least once each budget cycle; redistribute income; provide the government with a spending limitation; and provide transparency by which the government may be held accountable at the end of each budget cycle or political term.

The budget is generally composed of an operating budget, which shows expenditures for the current period, and a capital budget which shows the financial plans for long-term capital improvements, facilities, and equipment. The two budgets may be consolidated in order to indicate the amount of total estimated revenues available for the current period and the amount of new debt to be incurred for projects in the capital budget. For more information on expected incomes, see Local Revenue Structures.

Process

Although details on the budgeting process vary significantly from city to city, there are four main sequential stages in the lifecycle of a public budget:

i. Preparation

    Involves the development of expenditure estimates for departments in light of available revenues.

ii. Approval

    Budget estimates are then submitted to a city council or board for review and modification, often with citizen input from public meetings. The budget is then legally approved and adopted.

iii. Implementation

    The budget is then implemented by municipal departments throughout the year.

iv. Evaluation/Audit

    The performance of all governmental units is monitored and measured throughout the fiscal year. Those indicators are evaluated at the end of the year to inform the budget process for the following year.

Authority

The entity that prepares the budget may be a mayor with independent authority to develop and make recommendations for the budget to the city council. In other cases, a city manager may initiate the process then the mayor may review and comment on the budget for the council. In all cases, the council is solely responsible for approving the budget. Once the proposed budget is approved through a budget ordinance, the newly adopted plan becomes a legally binding document for the mayor or city manager to administer. After the fiscal year has been completed, most state laws and municipal charters require an independent financial audit which is made public.

Requirements

In addition, state laws dictate that nearly all cities operate under balanced-budget requirements, meaning that cities almost always plan on ending the fiscal year with a surplus to carry forward. This ending balance is often referred to as a "reserve" or "rainy day fund," which is often capped in size, and becomes available revenue for the next fiscal year, as is the case in two-thirds of states. In other states, the fund is maintained to use only in times of unexpected revenue shortfalls or budget deficits. Eight states refund the money to the taxpayers, and nine states earmark the funds.

TAXES

Local Revenue Structures

Since local governments are corporations of state government, local revenue structures are largely determined by state doctrine. While state governments generally aim to provide sufficient autonomy and support to local governments, there are fifty state-local revenue systems that even vary within states. In this case, autonomy refers to the amount of authority a municipality has over its ability to initiate or modify the types and amounts of revenue it receives.

A local revenue structure is influenced by a municipality's size, geography, metro type, land use, and coverage of government services. Other local determinants include numerous legal, political, and economic influences, including historical precedent, national economic trends, federal mandates, state laws, intergovernmental relations, regional precedent, citizens' preferences, and the city administration's preferences. Additionally, the municipality's political policies towards new growth, social welfare, and business competition are reflected in its revenue structure.

Revenue from Taxes

Taxes are an essential source of revenue for all levels of government. Like other parts of the revenue structure, tax revenue set by municipalities is restricted by state governments. States are not uniform in their approach to allowing municipalities to utilize the three major sources of tax revenue - property, sales, and income taxes - usually permitting some combination.

In some states, municipalities receive revenue from two of these taxes, usually some combination of property and sales taxes. Additionally, some states assign a portion of state tax revenues to those municipalities with a substantial share of the state population (New York City, St. Louis, and Kansas City, for example). Municipalities in other states are reliant on one tax with only a limited degree of reliance on a second. And in other states, municipalities rely on only one revenue source, usually the property tax. Municipalities in this latter category are either heavily reliant on that one source (as in Connecticut), or that one source is a relatively low percentage of total general revenues (Idaho).

Revenue from Other Sources

In order to bolster revenue, there are several other revenue sources, including local option taxes, service charges, and fees levied by municipalities, counties, or special district governments with state approval. These additional sources help municipalities, especially smaller cities, gain financial stability, broaden the tax base, expand the types of activities taxed, and increase their independence from state and federal finances.

Revenue from Intergovernmental Transfers

Intergovernmental transfers are transfers of funds from one level of government to another. This may be done to fund general government operations or for specific purposes.

Similar to a year or so earlier when I opened my LinkedIn page and noticed a similar profile belonging to Vincent Coyle. It was easy for me to look at his profile and immediately recognize his face. I saw how accomplished he was on his profile and then decided to take a shot and contact him, although I suspected that someone had hacked his page. Shortly after, he sent a reply and asked me to send him my vision. I had one vision to help educate young black males on how the justice system works and what it is like to go through the system (prison) as a means of deterrence and prevention.

I was at this time trying to smooth over the public outcry amidst a brewing chaos over the killing of unarmed black men. I was working with black men who knew they had no chance of dealing with cops once arrested and chose to stand up for their rights. I mean the jails and the courts would not help. I knew the police are not trained to retreat or prevent rather to protect and serve, and the best strategy to bring understanding of the system was using film, plays, my books, and organizations. This would help educate people about the system and how not to become a suspect. Technically, it is nearly impossible if you're black because of the history of the justice system, and racism. Up to this point I had struggled to get any support even from people who knew me best and had been in the streets and should have showed they cared.

After sharing my vision with Vincent Coyle, I became very anxious for his response. It was trying to catch a big fish and needed bigger bait but didn't have any available. Three days later he replied and said he'd be happy to help but first I had to get the right people behind me and help them to see my vision. He mentioned the group Faith and Politics who had been on a pilgrimage in Derry Northern Ireland. The group had managed to invite John Lewis and other key political and faith leaders to commemorate the Civil Rights struggle of Northern Ireland, ahead of the 50th anniversary of both Selma and Bloody Sunday.

Vincent shared his admiration for the work I was doing, which was bigger than the community. I shared with him that my goal was raising 75k, but he said I required a million. He offered to link my work to the work he was doing and offer his full support. Upon closer study of his work, I came across reconciliation and that is when it struck me that I could use reconciliation in my community and the world over.

I was in over my head with connecting the U.S. Civil Rights leader with the U.S. Civil Rights champions (Dr. Martin Luther King, John Lewis, Rev. Jessie Jackson, Al Sharpton, and others) who had carried the torch for persecuted communities across the country. I discovered that Dr. King's son, Martin Luther King Jr. III had been in Derry Northern Ireland honoring the Civil Rights leaders, through the Faith and Politics group from Washington DC, an organization that hosts pilgrimages for political leaders across the world.

Corporate executives, faith leaders, and John Lewis had been on the pilgrimage in Northern Ireland, and recognized John Hume and the Civil Rights leaders throughout Northern Ireland. I reached out to the group and notified them that Vincent was coming to the U.S., and to the South to work with me ahead of the unrest and police brutality stirring in the U.S.

It only took one phone call for him to get through to the administration, yet I had tried unsuccessfully for six months. I remember when Vincent arrived he asked me to get the mayor on the phone, and I told him I didn't know the mayor so I couldn't get him on the phone. Connections are powerful because the next day the mayor was standing on the State House steps with us, hosting the first ever Day of Reconciliation. Not to mention that he was still encouraged even after we notified him that the local chapter of the NAACP, had been reached out to profile our meetings. I was taken aback but I guess activism has its dangers. We visited all white churches and all black churches and were welcomed warmly even after challenging the status quo and separation.

I ended up visiting several Irish pubs, Catholic churches, Hibernian's hunts, Irish famine sites, the United Nation Irish artifacts among others during this time.

VINCENT COYLE

Little did I know that months later I would be among attendees at the UN opening 71st General assembly, and in church with the Secretary General standing in front of several black civil service agents. When Vincent invited me to take a picture with the Secretary General and the Heads of the Catholic churches, I couldn't even get my arm up steadily because I was nervous. There was a great record and history of the work Vincent had undertaken in Ireland. I spent two weeks with Vincent Coyle in Midtown New York hotels where he delivered his speeches, and he was respected because of his own civil rights struggles.

Watching the kind of response that Vincent had for blacks got me thinking of the transformational change that would impact my community if our eyes were opened up to this truth, and I immediately knew I would be telling the story of reconciliation for some time. Vincent in his speech said that 'if you're black in America and you fear whites, you at least know who your enemy is, and if you're Irish in Ireland your enemy could look just like you and prolong your battle to nearly hundreds of years - No blacks, No Irish and No dogs'.

Learning about The Irish Famine and the Irish slaves to the U.S. were even more surprising, as well as the Mural of Solidarity in Northern Ireland by the Bogside artist known all around the world. At this point the Derry flag at the SC State of Reconciliation Day meant more, now that I knew the history of the Irish struggle. I recognized the Irish who had died in the canals of Columbia, SC and whose monument was erected during one of the worst floods in the area. State President James Lawracy, was a key figure in mobilizing support for the Irish and it gave me much pride to watch Father Michael say the Irish blessing that day. Jim has since become the State

President of the Ancient Order of Hibernians, and done exceptionally well in getting the Irish community story out.

Everyone has a historical background and is capable of making a difference to another person's life. It is this realization that supports the pride that the Irish and Scottish possess in their history. At the end of it all I ended up joining 10 thousand Irishmen and women that afternoon at a Celtic fest spearheaded by Jim and Vincent. I could not believe I was one of the few blacks but for once I did not feel black. I didn't even feel the tension while among the white police officers, the kind I felt when I attended predominately white events. The event involved prayers by the Bishop from Bible Way Baptist Church, followed by SC State Choir singing Amazing Grace and thereafter the National Anthem. The Irish had something that connected their struggle.

We added an Agenda and Proclamation and a Performance by P-Dash who had videoed a song about George Stinney. Stinney was a 14-year-old, 90 lbs. black kid electrocuted by the State of South Carolina on charge of murdering two little white girls. Unfortunately, it was later established that he was too small to have killed the girls and moved their bodies with a bike bigger than him from the location of the crime to where the bike was found. Tom Mullikin had helped one of his lawyer friends on the case and had even aided the Pilgrimage that led to a historic Freedom Ride to Mother Emanuel Church with Senator Clementa Pinckney. In 2015, Senator Pinckney was assassinated at the Charleston Church Massacre at Mother Emanuel Church.

We even paid our respects to the funeral of Eric Washington who was killed by his friends. WIS-TV anchor Lionel Moise broke the story of Vincent Coyle's work in Reconciliation and the connection with my book, the Civil Rights Movements in Ireland and the United States. As monumental as the moment was, Ben Cochran and myself who were active in helping with the campaign understood that the news would have been great if we had political ambition. However, we were more concerned with the community and the people who cared and got involved in reconciliation efforts.

Carole Murray a long-time radio host in the community was a pioneer in breaking the story of reconciliation through her mostly conservative radio show. It bodes well with my initiative since my return to the community would be acknowledged, and even more leverage was that Carole was a part of the making of Billy Graham's film and a part of My Hope Project.

Martin Crosthwaite was a key figure in integrating large, small and influential churches around my community. The reception was overwhelmingly positive as Congregations stated that that was the best service in years.

The pride of the black community that day was refreshing as Capa performed the theme song, 'No Right Way to Do Wrong'. Big Ben a successful event organizer and activist was the proud voice of community organizing. I recall this event with satisfaction and thinking about it today, it is interesting to see the progress. For example, James Lawracy is now State President of the Ancient Order of Hibernians leading national events all over the world and in Ireland, while the Mayor of Columbia Steve Benjamin is now the President of the City of Mayors organization of all the City Mayors. Steve Benjamin was a very active voice in politics and leading fights for the Democratic Party which was helping to build a base in the urban community. Steve is a great asset as a graduate of University of South Carolina, and former Student Government President who carried the weight among the elite for both races. He is now headed for a National Role in Politics and Business.

It seemed that every celebration was a way of life that could save us all. It was bigger than the monuments, but the living monuments were fortified and built on relationships, and this was powerful. There was Irish history in Camden South Carolina just behind Tom Mullikin's Law firm, which was represented by a statue of Reconciliation. Tom had since become State Director for the Billy Graham Evangelical Association. Vincent and I had visited the monument while he was in the U.S. on tour where he paid his respects.

A local journalist and Time writer Rachel Haney a good friend of Betty Malone, had been referenced as attending the South Carolina Philharmonic ahead of the USC Women's historic run the next year. In 2017, A'ja Wilson led The University of South Carolina to the NCAA tournament title and she became the first pick in the WNBA draft and won rookie of the year.

South Carolina was on a roll winning 3 of the 4 National tournaments in sports but was also riddled with police brutality and white supremacy from Mother Emanuel Church with Senator Clementa Pinckney murdered to Walter Scott when a trooper shot the suspect in broad day light after just asking him to show his driver's license. He made National news after the victim's body cam provided evidence where he asked why he had shot him. The officer's response was he suspected that he was reaching out for a gun not a wallet. Jail house tapes that surfaced later showed the same officer saying he didn't have any problems with niggers in the Midwest. He said they don't fear niggers in the South, rather they keep or have kept them in check. Even Governor, Nikki Haley noted that the fact that there was no riot in South Carolina after the Mother Emanuel Church shooting was a ray hope for a better future. The church understood that they could not get any form of support even if they protested and so they responded in love and not with the usual historical lynching.

I organized a video shoot to promote our production using the South Carolina State House as a backdrop, as opposed to protesting. This displayed the community as being proactive towards prevention. Vincent perceived the vision and Justice Inform and the International Day of reconciliation were birthed.

The more I shared about the cause, the more I met whites who mentioned that they had problems too if not more than blacks and expressed the need to expand the cause. Eventually Billy Graham Evangelical Association supported Reconciliation Day at the SC State House by sending dozens of supporters during the film. Tons of churches and families embraced the work we were doing, and we even got support and invites to Chicago and other local areas. Most were either affected by drugs, crime, violence, jails, and or prisons. The support for juvenile intervention took us from house to house, family to family, jail to jail, and prison to prison as the quest progressed.

MAGNA CARTA 800TH

Vincent returned to Ireland to carry on with his international work as I travelled to Bloomberg, while Gavin Serkin made his way to South Carolina. A year or so later I awoke to the news that I could expand further interest on Emerging Markets in my community through Vincent Coyle.

Vincent Coyle had introduced me to Gavin whom he had met in his travels in countries across the world. I made a call to Vincent, who had given Gavin my book on the eve of Magna Carta 800th celebration. It was a celebration by the American Bar Association which attracted its nearly 400,000 worldwide memberships. The event was attended by the Queen Elizabeth, Princess William and Prince Harry. Then Attorney General Loretta Lynch spoke ahead of her official appointment as an Attorney General, the next week. William Hubbard, partner at Nelson, Riley, Mullins and Scarborough the largest firm in South Carolina and Top 100th largest in the United States, was the President of the American Bar Association, and also Chairman of the Board of Directors for the World Justice Project. World Justice Project was an independent multidisciplinary organization working to advance the rule of law worldwide. His office was a block from the SC State Capitol, and I had met him at an awards event earlier that was honoring Death Penalty Advocate Diana Holt and her efforts appealing death penalty cases.

Holt had a successful career turn after serving a sentence of five years' probation, for a botched armed robbery as undercover FBI agent with her then boyfriend. The boyfriend was charged and sentenced in this case. She had also recently won a release for Edward Lee Elmore, an African American on death row for the 1982 murder of a wealthy white widow in Edwards's hometown of Greenwood, South Carolina. I spoke to both Diana and Hubbard that night alongside other high-profile lawyers, judges, prosecutors and law makers who touted Diana's resilience. Diana was a recent feature in the CNN Death Row Stories, and subject of Anatomy of Injustice: A Murder Case Gone Wrong. This was a book by Raymond Bonner about Holt's work on the Lemore case. I introduced myself to Hubbard and spoke briefly about my book 'Finding Me', and my work in racial reconciliation which had gained the attention of International Reconciliation Campaigner Vincent Coyle. Hubbard spoke about his work on the reconciliation program but could not disclose more about it.

I later thought of arranging a meeting with Hubbard and Vincent Coyle after hearing about the ceremonial event in London. I was with Vincent during the European Tour of my book 'Finding Me' which had advanced all over Europe, including France, Venice, and Monaco. I also advertised the book before writers, directors, and film festival attendees ahead of the Cannes Film Festival, and The Grand Prix race in Monaco, where it would be presented to Gavin Serkin whose book Frontier: The Top 10 Emerging Markets of Tomorrow was highly reviewed. The strong reviews of Gavin's book were because of his stance on the Rule of Law and addressing of the legal framework on investment, and corruption at the highest level of investment.

After the event, I made a call to Hubbard and delivered copies of my book and promo shirts to his office that could be used at our State House event. Vincent and Hubbard met at the Eve of the Magna Carta Celebration and took a picture together, while sharing words of encouragement and congratulations for Hubbard's success. Vincent, Gavin, Hubbard and I arranged to meet, and Hubbard was given a copy of Gavin's book, Frontier: The Top 10 Emerging Markets of Tomorrow, considering his interest in the Rule of Law. The Rule of Law was more in question as the campaign and issues were heating up under the Trump and Russia investigation.

It had been over a decade since I had learned that war was the casualty of finance, and I could only vaguely remember the details since I began my study of the financial market. My return home had been focused on the criminal justice side of activism, as I couldn't think of any other plight facing blacks besides police brutality, criminal justice system incarceration and related issues. I had forgotten the connection between crime and finances as this was camouflaged in the urban community by other complexities such as drugs, violence etc. Since the abolition of slavery the community has turned into a crime scene, breaking down aspects such as jobs, employment, health, Medicare service, etc.

The fact that the community barely survives, much less creates a tax paying base was a major concern. All this time I had no idea that these guys had seen it all except for Vincent. As I read Gavin's book I knew that there was much more to finance and especially journalism. I could only imagine the stories that didn't get told, and this was a well-funded book through Bloomberg data. Unbeknownst to me, Gavin, Vincent and I had a common ground, as we were linking crime, corruption, poverty and opportunity for education in finances. They had seen the worst of human suffering and conditions from all over the world. However, the problem with my efforts was that in a developed world, the opportunity people see doesn't highlight the underlying suffering. I hoped that this would change, except it was going to take extra clarity to get some high-profile personalities which could be a challenge. There was yet another challenge since South Carolina had the worst Headlines over the last three years featuring shootings, killings and a massacre of blacks.

BLOOMBERG

Arriving at Bloomberg Offices in New York was a major feat, fresh off a peak of getting a tweet and picture of Gavin reading my book in Spain by the ocean side. I found out later that he loves surfing and being able to balance business and pleasure which was a great advantage!

New York already was and is still a buzz of energy and my hopes were rising. Not to mention that I loved New York for the simple fact that everybody was busy doing their business and nobody was in anyone's business. I would describe New York as the grind and hustle epicenter that screams 'anything can happen at any time'. Understanding New York from the world views covers up the fact that it is just an idea built on top of ideas, soaring up in modernity and technological advancement.

New York is a big 24/7 show that draws the world's attention and sells itself over and over again. It's the only place you can be ordinary and great at the same time. It's the living show on a TV set, where you can take a picture in Times Square or Brooklyn and demand the attention of the world. It's the big city of dreams and if you are not in New York you're just driving and striving. I was eager to see if New York would make it happen for me.

Meeting Gavin downstairs at Bloomberg was exciting. I was hoping I could get a pass up to see him. The ladies at the front desk were not allowing me to get a pass, rather they buzzed Gavin to let him know I was waiting. Gavin threw his jacket over his shoulder and made it easier for me to relax. I was nervous until I saw how easily he took his jacket off and I buttoned mine every so often. Next we exited the office and ended up drinking suds at an Irish bar - compliments to Irishman Vincent Coyle.

Gavin made a call to Vincent and other men he'd met along the way as he travelled and who had left no country unturned. Vincent himself had championed reconciliation across the world and had met me while traveling to the State Capitol in South Carolina to host the first ever day of international reconciliation. A few suds down, Gavin got bird droppings on his jacket which helped me relax even more and made the meeting even easier.

I told Gavin that being black it was easier getting shot down in the Middle of 5th Ave. or where we were at Midtown, and in 30 minutes my life would not matter. By this time, I had unbuttoned my jacket and spoke about all the books I'd written and how I wanted to give him a copy personally signed by me. Gavin on the other hand passed me a copy of his latest Live Bloomberg TV presentation and this got me floating on Irish clouds. The day got brighter and cooler and his wife Jules found us at Midtown drinking and enjoying our conversations. We took a few pictures, but I felt like I had missed the moment with the world's most important man. I learned that any time you have a connection with data released by Bloomberg you gained a different status because this data is utilized by institutions and institutional investors in management of investment accounts, 401 k, retirement, city and government accounts, as well as major purchases of government securities etc.

Gavin was gone and I was jumping back into my personal car, which was being driven by my best friend, who 20 years earlier had driven me while on the streets. The only difference from 20 years earlier was that I was going back to a hotel alone with Gavin's signed book. He had signed it, while he, Jules and myself were together in downtown New York and I was still elated, still broke, but highly elated.

Feeling unaccomplished after the first meeting with Gavin I begged Vincent for a second chance to meet Gavin to pour out my heart and he agreed. I called Gavin and he gave me a time and place for the meeting. The next day I arrived and got out of my car on the curb of 54th in Midtown Bloomberg Offices, and I was stunned to see Gavin and Jules wearing my promotional shirts in downtown New York. Everyone along the streets could not believe Gavin when he told them I was the star in this movie. I agreed to be the star and garnered my courage to straight up tell him I needed help because I was a black man in America, at risk of being shot and forgotten in 30 minutes or locked up for 30 years because I had no value. I explained to him that because there was no economic value invested in my life, to make someone come to my aid the odds were not statistically high.

Gavin asked what his role was, and I confidently said economics, because he had the power to add economic value to my life. He shared with me about the billion-dollar success stories that were being implemented in Africa and abroad. These were places where economic inclusion was attractive for wealthy investors who were in telecommunication like Safaricom and Vodafone. These investments were connecting people to wealth and opportunity, and executives knew this and were happy to join and work with him. Jules looked at Gavin, put her hand behind his back and told him that she would love to visit South Carolina the next time they were in the U.S. It was at this point the magic happened. I had forgotten that I had a car waiting 20 blocks away and had to walk to my room, where I was not able to get even a wink of sleep, though I was tired. On my flight back I opened Gavin's book to read and observed that his story was similar to what I was working out.

I took out my book and searched for the section where I had written about the 12 years I had studied the financial markets from the Wall Street Journal, financial analysis among others. I discovered that it actually showed where the money went, and this was by meeting people like Gavin who knew where the money was. It seemed that every page I turned referenced a community like my own where fund managers and people like Gavin explored to find new opportunities. They were in search of returns, what would make them successful investors in markets, and their next community investment or the country that proved its worth. Now I had to figure out how and where it would be. It was not SC because we were one of the last states economically, at least for blacks and the plight of slavery prior not to mention the poorest after the civil war. It was a state that came to be because most southern states worked blacks for free labor which was cheap labor, and when this ended the blacks became taxpayers though the labor was still cheap and they faced discretionary discrimination from whites for jobs and in the distribution of funds amongst other related economic disparities.

DARLA MOORE SCHOOL OF BUSINESS

I recall watching as the flags at Darla Moore School of Business were about to change. I took Gavin's book with me and met a black man on campus that looked out of place. He came up to me and asked if he could help me. I learned later that he was the Dean of Doctoral Studies. My interest was however on every individual on the campus and when I gave him Gavin's book, he said he could connect me with a professor who would be interested in introducing me to his students. That would prove to be an achievement because Dr. Colin Jones kept his word.

Weeks later Gavin, the professor and I were on the phone. It was at this point I started feeling like somebody, only to find out later that they had reached out to Gavin asking him who I was and why I was representing him. What they did not understand was that Gavin had travel experiences deeper than a black man on the streets in the south.

I had no idea that my platform could benefit Bloomberg, Gavin or Wiley Finance thus I wasn't about to ask for funding. Later I discovered that connections were a full circle of value. At this point I became interested in the value of the institutions I was working with. The bigger picture was that I was a connection for Bloomberg, Bloomberg Author, Bloomberg Head of International Desk of Emerging Markets, and with Darla Moore School of Business, a school in the State of South Carolina and one that ranked low in the economic poll. Such extreme disparities do not present any opportunity to connect, but a few years later the Secretary General of the UN was invited to the University of South Carolina. Remember that Nikki Haley, former Governor of South Carolina was Head of United Nations for the United States, under the Trump Administration. A year later after his work in South Carolina Gavin took up a position with Frontier Funds, and this would give him unlimited mobility, to recruit billionaires away from the desk of Bloomberg who would lead investments in Africa, India, China, Korea, Cuba, Turkey, and Iran among others.

The event at Darla Moore School of Business was a success, as we hit it off with staff and faculty just as we had in New York. This led to a good response by all participants, topped off by eager students. The business community missed out on the opportunity because there was a challenge in the marketing efforts which would have informed the state about the presence of financial leader Gavin. The urban community professionals were in attendance and the word was getting out to reach the communities and small business, and entrepreneurs.

The panel discussion and book signing event with Gavin didn't take long. However, there were numerous questions on the country, finance and policy from the inspired young future leaders. All these young people would one day reference Gavin in their work since he was the pinnacle in their field. Looking back just a few weeks ago and recalling walking up several steps in the hope of salvation for the endless journey for finance, I got an opportunity to invite one the most powerful men in finance to South Carolina. Surely this was the Wall Street bond we needed.

The next phase of events was looking at each other in the full realization of the value and benefits of crossing barriers. South Carolina was now on its way up, but it seemed that my community was not yet close to redemption.

Later we hosted the top 10 scholars from the prestigious Darla Moore International School of Business at the Sony Club of New York. This led to the school topping the list as an International Business Major school, holding the first position and retaining the position for 17 years.

EMERGING MARKETS BOOTCAMP

(Bloomberg Emerging Markets Boot Camp New York)

Earlier that morning I attended a Boot Camp in Bloomberg with 500 of the top managers in the world on Emerging Market work. It was at this conference planned by Gavin and his team, that I saw the Bloomberg machine in action.

It was a feat to hear about the fears and challenges these top financial journalists faced as they brought the stories from tough areas to the marketplace. During their work they showed how money would funnel in and change the landscape, eventually producing democracies and opportunity for everyone. All this took place sometimes even under the fear of death. Gavin himself had witnessed beheadings and also been detained during assignment.

Gavin Serkin @GSerkin 4h

Reconciliation in South Carolina front page news @terrencegallman @VincentCoyle1

jules serkin @julesserkin

@GSerkin author catch…

Gavin referenced Vincent and I on a tweet where he was pictured reading the front page news of the Wall Street Journal in New York on Wall Street, before his Wall Street Journal interview with Dan Keller. This was at the height of the removal of the Confederate flag from the South Carolina State House, just after a self-radicalized white supremacist killed Clemente Pinckney, a prominent Senator and pastor of Mother Emanuel Church alongside eight other parishioners while injuring scores of people. Debate blazed across South Carolina and garnered international interest more so on racial relations. Vincent and I had been working in South Carolina during reconciliation and helped prevent racial discords from going further. This was in the understanding that reconciliation is a vital part of moving communities forward in spite of the past.

Reconciliation was equally present at Wall Street considering that investment is a recipient of reconciliation – when people get along, investments flow. If South Carolina was to empower its citizens, then institutional investors needed to be attracted to the urban communities, thus the place of reconciliation. However, during this time President Trump had put immigration on hold, directly affecting labor wages in South Carolina. Blacks were priced out of the market and subsequently this affected whites, since local opportunities were marginalized by the burgeoning Hispanic business owners and working class. Once again blacks failed to attract institutional investment directly into their community.

In-spite of budding cities replicating the Silicon Valley of the South, beginning with the flow of Angel Investors reinventing the community with modern offices and pushing tech and modern businesses and related developments, blacks are still not tech driven. South Carolina instead was leading in international and national news for having the worst tragedies in the decade next to the Michael Brown shooting.

During this meeting I communicated personal responsibility as a means to deterrence. I was still striving to bring in a flood of investments to change this landscape even with my Justice Inform campaign and book Finding Me memoir, against all odds. However, if it was no match, I needed financial markets to be in our favor. Gavin and Vincent both knew the plight of blacks against the whites in the South, but also knew I was no match for the discretionary discrimination that still occurred and would occur even after the international stage of Bloomberg and the United Nations, nevertheless I remained committed.

MOTHER EMANUEL CHURCH

We arrived in Charleston to pick Gavin and Jules up for the Sunday service at Mother Emanuel Church. This is where nine black parishioners had been killed during a bible study by Dylan Roof, a self-radicalized white supremacist.

Dr. Novel Goff, the presiding Pastor, accepted a token from Northern Ireland, and Dr. King Church choir that had traveled from Atlanta sung alongside Mother Emanuel choir. The token was given on behalf of John Hume, Ivan Cooper, and The City of Derry who were inspired by Dr. King and the U.S. Civil Rights Movement.

UNITED NATIONS

I wasn't too offended the next year as the Secretary General Ban Ki Moon and a host of World Dignitaries toured the United Nations. We spent time in prayer with Cardinal Theodore McCarrick, one of the highest ranked U.S. Clergy, and archbishop of Washington at the Holy Church ahead of the Pope's visit. His resignation had been accepted by Pope Francis for sexual misconduct dating back over 50 years after discovering mounting payoffs to victims. The vigil at the Holy Church in New York was a solemn moment surrounded by an entourage of high-profile clergy men and women. Little did I know this prestigious event had hidden skeletons that would rock the world for as many generations as the scorned victims.

I watched Vincent interact with the clergy on the highest level with his well-developed skills and networking abilities. Notwithstanding, he was in the U.S. while a storm of Bloody Sunday meetings requiring his attention happened on the forefront back in Ireland. We spent days and nights at the UN and early morning checking in with Ireland. Vincent was Chief Steward of the Bloody

Sunday March and was steadily falling out with its leadership. Not to mention that while we planned support for the movie I had aspired to make, this very leadership assumed that Vincent was utilizing their platform to raise millions of dollars in the U.S. which was not true. Vincent's visit to the U.S. was because no one had invested a dime in Justice Inform and Reconciliation, and he thought he could help my cause. He never at any given time charged or raised a dime. Later he went on a world tour to Japan, China, Korea, and South America, and these countries represented interests worth millions. However, from South Carolina to New York there was no interest in giving even a dime except to Blue Lives Matter.

At the United Nations level the Irish Consulate and others were more than generous during our tour and meetings. Vincent knew the level of skill needed to navigate and bring attention to our cause - Justice Inform, and the Long Walk to Reconciliation. At the same time there were extreme protests going on outside the United Nations and all over Midtown. Protests that were nothing compared to Trump protests since they were few in number.

We went from church with the United Nations Secretary General Ban Ki Moon to the World Premier of HUMAN by Yann Arthus Bertrand, legendary film maker. His trio of films Good Planet, Planet Earth, and Human enjoy billions of views, not to mention that his latest film was made from over 2000 testimonies in 10 years across 60 continents showing the vast differences of our lives and how we are alike. This happened one meeting ahead of the Pope's visit, President Obama, Facebook Founder Mark Zuckerberg, Leonardo DiCaprio amongst others, during the release of Sustainable Development Goals that included Climate Change. It was followed by Beyoncé and more headliners at the Central Park Concert.

It was feat to be seated in the United Nations among world leaders. The rich collection of artifacts that encompass the United

Nations, from turmoil and conflict around the world to bomb debris made into sculptures to the Irish Slave Ship.

The world premiere of HUMAN afterparty overlooked the Hudson and New Jersey skyline. We were interviewed by a host of entertainment and news correspondents. One in particular was with the infamous Tanisha LaVerne Grant, the goto for Entertainment Affairs. This provided an opportunity for the Urban Community since she represented HUMAN, a story that held so many stories and could contribute to the ongoing fight between Africans and Americans. The learning curve would increase tremendously, and it was a great time for Vincent Coyle to start off the Big Conversation by asking what makes us HUMAN, and how Reconciliation is the best start for humanity. It is a conversation that attracted the interest of presidents and world leaders even as Emma Freud and a host of other celebrity professionals took to the red carpet. Ironically Trump Towers stands tall at a corner just opposite from the United Nations building.

Back to the party at the United Nations where there were thousands of people in business. Homeland Security on the other hand was nothing short of a bust, not to mention we ended up in a room that had surveillance and technology that possibly could analyze thoughts. The atmosphere was great as we met with Lenni Montiel at United Nations, the Assistant Secretary-General for Economic and Social Affairs, and UNDP Deputy Regional Director Latin America and Caribbean.

We also met Michael O'Neill, United Nations Assistant Secretary-General and the Director of External Relations, and Advocacy in the United Nations Development Programme. Not to mention that a year or so later we were on tour through the State House in South Carolina led by the then Governor, Nikki Haley who led the removal of the Confederate flag from the SC State House Grounds, after the tragic shooting at Mother Emanuel. Today Nikki Halley is the United States

Ambassador to the United Nations under President Trump. We also met with Ravi, a huge campaigner for gender equality who is known all over the world. UNICEF, a key contributor to world issues was also well represented.

The commemoration and memorial of 9/11 held prior to the Pope's arrival was nothing short of breathtaking. We stood downtown with the Captain of Firehouse 10 who were the first responders to the scene of the terrorist attack. It was an attack that killed nearly 3000 people. Fire House 10 is situated a hundred yards from the scene. We were also honored to meet with the Chaplain who gave the last rights to the victims of the attack.

Next were other meetings held in New York that contrasted with the rest of the world. We were given a 9/11 pennant by the captain of Firehouse 10 and were able to give a token of appreciation to the Captain on behalf of the Irish Leadership. I recall how when our work on reconciliation began, Prince Charles and Queen Elizabeth traveled to Northern Ireland for reconciliation over a decade after the murder of his uncle Lord Mountbatten.

At St. Patrick Cathedral we got kicked out for being a distraction to the Cardinal and ahead of the historic visit of the Pope. This was because Vincent, a Game of Thrones Actor was recognized by the children from an affluent family while in the church, and they went to take pictures with him. However, he later took pictures with the African Cardinal bishop, who probably one day would be the first black Pope.

EMPEA AND INTERNATIONAL
MONETARY FUND

(Gavin Serkin Keynote EMPEA and IFC GPEC with WSJ Dan Keller)

During the Global Private Equity Conference hosted by EMPEA and IFC where Gavin Serkin was the Keynote speaker I sat on a seat I was not supposed to occupy. The seat was reserved for the Chairman of the EMPEA and his elects.

EMPEA was home to over 300 Companies whose interest was in investing in Emerging Markets and had over 2000 member companies with over 1 trillion U.S. dollars under its management.

The Global Private Equity Conference on the other hand is the leading emerging markets private equity event in the world, which convenes over 850 investment professionals from more than 60 countries annually. The conference attracts a wide array of industry practitioners drawn from family offices, private and public pension funds, foundations, endowments, insurance companies, development finance institutions, fund-of-funds, established global fund managers, new investors, international and national government officials and regulators, to private equity consultants and advisors. They convene for thought-provoking discussions, debates and analyses that are top-of-mind for business today and valuable to industry leaders.

IFC, a member of the World Bank Group, is the largest global development institution focused exclusively on the private sector in developing countries. IFC utilizes and leverages its products and services, as well as products and services of other institutions in the World Bank Group, to provide development solutions customized to its clients' needs. IFC applies its financial resources, technical expertise, global experience, and innovative thinking to help its partners overcome financial, operational, and political challenges. Clients view IFC as a provider and mobilizer of scarce capital, knowledge, and long-term partnerships that can help address critical constraints in areas such as finance, infrastructure, employee skills, and the regulatory environment. IFC is also a leading mobilizer of third-party resources for its projects. Its willingness to engage in difficult environments and its leadership in crowding-in private finance enable the organization to extend its footprint and have a development impact beyond its direct resources.

EMPEA is a global industry association for private capital in emerging markets. As an independent non-profit organization, the association's membership comprises 300+ firms representing institutional investors, fund managers and industry advisors, who together manage more than US$5 trillion in assets across 130 countries. EMPEA's members share the organization's belief that private capital is a highly suited investment strategy in emerging markets, with a unique ability to deliver attractive long-term investment returns and promote the sustainable growth of companies and economies.

In support of its mission, EMPEA researches, analyzes and disseminates authoritative information on emerging markets, private capital fundraising, investment and exits while continuously monitoring and reporting on industry trends, benchmarks, best practices and market developments. Further, it convenes meetings and conferences around the world which provide its members, prospective investors, and other interested stakeholders with forums and opportunities to debate, network and learn about key issues affecting private capital investing in emerging countries. Also, EMPEA collaborates with industry partners, including national and regional venture capital/private equity associations, to strengthen the network and knowledge base of emerging markets private capital practitioners; and advocates for policy and regulatory reforms that strengthen the environment for private capital investing in emerging markets.

Gavin's book is a faculty recommended reading by EMPEA to the like of Allen Greenspan, Former Fed Chief. While being interviewed by Dan Keller, Editor of Wall Street Journal, Gavin Serkin underlined the importance of Emerging Markets to investors and this covered Russia, North Korea, China and the number one subject Africa – a continent slated to take the lion's share of the market by 2050.

Hearing about Financial Inclusion was on my list with companies such as Acumen. Social good was the number one topic and it was highlighted that you could not sell your company unless you were engaged in it. The rise of tech had transcended many countries like Africa which were retaining more of their educated graduates unlike in the past.

The panels we led with institutional investors, policy makers, fund managers, general and limited partners of leading firms, journals and editors of news firms and organizations, covered investing insights into markets within their fields. All topics were related to the country or markets demographics, corruption, and economic indicators that were deemed for investment or selling. We concluded that reconciliation was the ability of people to get along, while justice inform focused on corruption and crime which threatens the stability of the investments. All these were issues I was dealing with in the U.S. and based on responsiveness held opportunities for investment.

There were more companies set up in the U.S. and focused on providing financial inclusion of the frontier market countries than in the U.S. or its urban communities. It was easy to follow the flow of technology and markets in other countries because of the rate of return. You could invest 100 million dollars in a developed country and hope to get 5 percent or invest 100 million dollars in a frontier market and get 100 percent return. There was no limit to the return even though it carried risks, but not withstanding the appetite for U.S. Dollars investors could develop the market especially in essential markets or goods.

There were few blacks who attended these events and the African or South Americans with dark skin usually were pitched or pitching themselves to everyone else. There was no need to connect or interact because it seems blacks and Africans could not fund each other for lack of market and or resources. I knew then there was an opportunity to bring the two to the market for investment and trade that could create new emerging markets. The urban community could then fund the frontier markets with capital and industry professionals that would lift the burden of poverty and raise the median household income. It would spur many new industries and technology which would aid and advance healthcare, transportation, communication and trade. This would open our markets to each other and increase innovation.

By the time Gavin and Dan Keller started with the questions, the EMPEA marketing team and I were tweeting away a storm from the event. I got so comfortable I started working with the camera man. Of course I was Gavin's media guy and Jules who was in London had spearheaded Gavin's social media activities. Together we managed to build up a hefty base of support with discussions running from slums to glass ceilings to his book, to prisons and presidents.

By the time Gavin came off stage I had secured the first interview as I sat on the reserved seat. It was a feat for our community having been right in the middle of the Private Equity Conference where publicizing the information was restricted to control information being misconstrued before it was channeled out right in the proper context. Gavin was surprised to see me as he walked off the stage.

Gavin covered events in Turkey that proceeded President Barack Obama, Nigeria and Africa's investment from the U.S. and President Obama's visits, restored the relationship with Cuba before Trump rescinded the agreements, and the historical trade agreements between India and Russia. He also highlighted conditions of North and South Korea and their economies, which have since led to the surprise negotiations with the U.S.

The presentation topics also included tips for global investing in growth markets, where Gavin Serkin identified Kenya, Myanmar, Romania, Argentina, Vietnam, Nigeria, Egypt, Saudi Arabia, Sri Lanka, and Ghana as the top emerging future markets. General trends were presented and discussed alongside promotion of health and innovation, clean energy, and strategies for economic growth.

I analyzed the participants at the conference and envisioned the impact on our investment and retirement accounts, if all were to be actively involved with the frontier markets. As I watched the list of supporters and the brand recognition, I optimistically held on to a dream that one day we would have similar support.

The agenda to help navigate the information and investment insights and opportunity, was the challenge set before me. I decided to create an intro course syllabus to emerging markets and investment, as it would help bridge the communities and the financial integration of urban communities. The subjects include:

1.   How and why money is created?

Money is any item or verifiable record that is generally accepted as payment for goods and services and repayment of debts, such as taxes, in a particular country or socio-economic context. The main functions of money are distinguished as: a medium of exchange, a unit of account, a store of value and sometimes, a standard of deferred payment.

Money derives its value by being declared by a government to be legal tender; that is, it must be accepted as a form of payment within the boundaries of the country for all debts - public and private.

Money can be used in a number of different ways. Your savings account provides you a safe place (a bank) to keep your money and gain interest on it while you are not using that money. But the money in your savings account does not sit in a giant vault in the bank, it is used to help other people buy homes and cars and go to college. When the bank makes a loan, it is drawing on all the money people have put into it. In this way the bank acts as a financial marketplace for money. A bank loan can help fuel growth but one day it will have to be paid back, with interest (a fee to cover the cost of borrowing).

2. How money circulates and the evolution into electronic transactions

The money supply of a country consists of currency (banknotes and coins) and, depending on the particular definition used there are one or more types of bank money (the balances held in checking accounts, savings accounts, and other types of bank accounts). Bank money, which consists only of records (mostly computerized in modern banking), forms by far the largest part of broad money in developed countries.

By the early 1990s, all transfers between banks and the Federal Reserve were done electronically. The three other important steps in the history of electronic money are;

i. Diners Club issued the first credit card in 1950. At first, credit cards were considered a special perk available mostly to rich businessmen. As soon as banks realized there were billions of dollars to be made by issuing credit to as many people as possible, credit cards exploded. Today's largest credit card company, Visa, started out as the Bank of America, and issued the BankAmericard in 1958. Today, there are over 200 million Visa cards in use in the United States alone.

ii. The Social Security Administration first offered automatic electronic deposit of money into bank accounts in 1975. Once people became comfortable with the concept of money being added to their accounts without ever holding the cash, the practice spread. People started paying bills, transferring money between accounts, and sending money electronically.

iii. The growing worldwide acceptance of the Internet has made electronic currency more important than ever before. Purchases can be made through a Website, with the funds drawn out of an Internet bank account, where the money was originally deposited electronically. In fact, economists estimate that only 8 percent of the world's currency exists as physical cash. The rest exists only on a computer hard drive, in electronic bank accounts around the world.

3. How government fiscal policy affects money

If a nation's economy were a human body, then its heart would be the central bank. And just as the heart works to pump life-giving blood throughout the body, the central bank pumps money into the economy to keep it healthy and growing. Sometimes economies need less money, and sometimes they need more. In this article, we'll discuss how central banks control the quantity of money in circulation.

The methods central banks use to control the quantity of money vary, depending on the economic situation and power of the central bank. In the United States, the central bank is the Federal Reserve, often called the Fed.

4. The value of money and how inflation devalues money

Most of the major economies around the world now use fiat currencies. Since they're not linked to a physical asset, governments have the freedom to print additional money in times of financial trouble. While this provides greater flexibility to address challenges, it also creates the opportunity to overspend.

The biggest hazard of printing too much money is hyperinflation. With more of the currency in circulation, each unit is worth less. While modest amounts of inflation are relatively harmless, uncontrolled devaluation can dramatically erode the purchasing power of consumers. If inflation reaches 5% annually, each individual's savings, assuming it doesn't accrue substantial interest, is worth 5% less than it was the previous year, which means it becomes harder to maintain the same standards of living. For this reason, central banks in developed countries usually try to keep inflation under control by indirectly taking money out of circulation when the currency loses value.

Regardless of the form it takes, all money has the same basic goals; i. which is to help encourage economic activity by increasing the market for various goods, and ii. enabling consumers to store wealth and therefore address long-term needs.

5. Global markets, financial markets and technical analysis

A financial market is a place where firms and individuals enter into contracts to sell or buy a specific product such as a stock, bond, or futures contract. Buyers seek to buy at the lowest available price and sellers seek to sell at the highest available price. There are a number of different kinds of financial markets, depending on what you want to buy or sell, but all financial markets employ professional people and are regulated.

If you want a loan or a savings account you would go to the bank or credit union, if you want to buy stock, a mutual fund or a bond you go to a securities market. The purpose of a securities market is primarily for businesses to acquire investment capital. Examples of securities markets include the New York Stock Exchange and the American Stock Exchange. However, there is another securities market known as the Over-the-Counter market, where a computer network of dealers, buy and sell shares.

6. Trade agreements

A trade agreement also known as trade pact, is a wide-ranging tax, tariff and trade treaty that often includes investment guarantees. It is through this treaty that two or more countries agree on terms that facilitate their trading with each other.

The most common trade agreements are of the preferential and free trade types. These are initiated to reduce or eliminate tariffs, quotas, and other trade restrictions on items traded between the signatories.

7. Stocks, futures and bonds

There are other markets in which people participate that you might not have thought about. These are called capital markets. Capital markets include the stock and the bond markets.

The markets are a source of financial capital for entrepreneurs who want to start businesses and for larger established businesses that want to expand. Capital markets bring together savers who want to invest with entrepreneurs and businesses that want to borrow.

Futures Contract

Futures markets provide a way for businesses to manage price risks. Buyers can obtain protection against rising prices and sellers can obtain protection against declining prices through futures contracts. For example, in spring, Farmer Jones planted 100 acres of soybeans and anticipated that in September he would harvest 5,000 bushels. His greatest concern is the price of soybeans in September whereby a fall in price leads to loss of money. To avoid this risk, Farmer Jones has his futures broker sell a contract for 5,000 bushels of soybeans for September at the current price. In this way the farmer locks in his September selling price. If the price is higher in September, the farmer will not make as much profit, but if the price has fallen, he will come out ahead. This process of obtaining price protection is called hedging.

8. Taxes that generate the foundations from the financial transactions

Tax is a fee charged/levied by a government on a product, income, or activity. If tax is levied directly on personal or corporate income, then it is a direct tax. If tax is levied on the price of a good or service, then it is called an indirect tax.

The purpose of taxation is to finance government expenditure. However, one of the most important uses of taxes is to finance public goods and services, such as street lighting and street cleaning. Since public goods and services do not allow a non-payer to be excluded, or allow exclusion by a consumer, there cannot be a market in the good or service, and so they need to be provided by the government or a quasi-government agency, which tend to finance themselves largely through taxes.

9. Global market analysis, private equity, and lobbyists

The global economy is the world economy or the worldwide economy. It is all the economies of the world which we consider as one economic system when pooled together, and simply put it is one giant entity. It is also the system of trade and industry across the world that has emerged due to globalization. In other words, it's the way in which countries' economies have been developing to operate collectively as one system.

Worldwide economic activity between various countries that are considered intertwined can affect other countries negatively or positively.

'We live in a global economy' is a common statement today. However, the question is when people use that phrase what exactly do they mean? Does it mean that any economic activity today occurs across the planet, whereas before it did not? Does it mean that all economic activities occur at a significantly faster pace than they used to? Observing giant multinational corporations there is a claim to having nationalities. However, their operations are global and national claims hollow because they form national allegiances as part of a marketing strategy in their home countries. In defining multinational corporations, these are companies that have businesses, staff, and premises in several countries.

According to Cooney, multinational companies love free trade agreements because they can then fire expensive workers in their home country and replace them with cheaper workers elsewhere. As more and more companies sell beyond their borders, the need for effective global marketing has also increased significantly. In definition global marketing refers to planning, producing or creating, placing, and promoting a company's products or services in the worldwide market.

10. How tariffs are used to affect global and domestic markets

Tariffs are used to restrict imports by increasing the price of goods and services purchased from overseas and making them less attractive to consumers. A specific tariff is levied as a fixed fee based on the type of item, for example, $1,000 on any car. An ad-valorem tariff is levied based on the item's value, for example, 10% of the car's value.

Governments may impose tariffs to raise revenue or to protect domestic industries, particularly nascent ones from foreign competition. By making foreign-produced goods more expensive, tariffs can make domestic production more attractive. This government approach is also known to protect jobs.

Tariffs can also be used as an extension of foreign policy i.e. imposing tariffs on a trading partner's main exports as a way to exert economic leverage.

11. Emerging and Frontier Markets

Frontier markets are less advanced capital markets in the developing world. Frontier markets are countries that are more established than the Least Developed Countries (LDCs), but still less established than the emerging markets. The markets are also known as "pre-emerging markets."

BREAKING DOWN 'Frontier Markets'

Investors pursue frontier, or pre-emerging, equity markets to seek potentially high returns. As many frontier markets do not have developed stock markets, investments are often private or direct in startups and infrastructure. Although it's possible to achieve strong results from investing in frontier markets, investors must also accept higher risks than in the United States or Europe, for example with the G7 nations.

Some of the risks investors face in frontier markets are political instability, poor liquidity, inadequate regulation, substandard financial reporting and large currency fluctuations. In addition, many markets are overly dependent on volatile commodities.

Frontier Markets and Lesser Developed Countries

Frontier markets are ahead of lesser developed countries although similar risks can apply for investors. The UN currently lists 47 lesser developed countries that face significant structural challenges to sustainable growth. This includes being extremely vulnerable to economic and environmental shocks leading to LDCs. LDCs access specific international support measures and financial aid, which are not available to more developed nations.

The CDP Secretariat of DPAD/DESA regularly reviews the status of LDCs to determine if and when they will graduate from the category. For example, in March 2018, the Committee for Development Policy (CDP) announced their recommendation that the nations of Bhutan, Kiribati, São Tomé and Príncipe and Solomon Islands should graduate from the LDC category.

Frontier Markets and Portfolio Management

Frontier market investments can have a low correlation to developed markets, and thus can provide additional diversification to an equity portfolio. In portfolio management investors must balance the strengths, weaknesses, opportunities and threats of certain choices, making tradeoffs and placing bets among debt, equity, domestic, international, growth, and safer options.

It's important to maximize a portfolio's return, given the investor's appetite for risk. Adding investments in frontier markets to a portfolio is not always suitable for certain investors. Those looking for stability, safety, and/or steady streams of income might stay clear of high-risk bets in these areas. However, if you do have the appetite and ability for risk (i.e. you can withstand losses in your portfolio), allocating a small portion of your assets to frontier markets could prove fruitful and add a new challenge.

Emerging markets will continue to drive global growth as they rotate their investments across foreign exchange, fixed income, equities, countries, and local currencies among other factors.

Over the last several decades emerging markets have grown and general market index in investments continues to cover this expansion.

Institutional investors in emerging markets buy debt on demand from their own populations for goods and services. The investment opportunities in emerging markets are centered around trade between these countries and the emergence of new industries such as travel and tourism among the middle class, and not with the developed world.

When it comes to technology the best opportunity in financial tech is getting more digitally advanced to access the opportunities of e-commerce and leverage on online business models.

Most institutional investors are best positioned to take advantage of other emerging markets transitions, such as the maturing of local bond markets, and potential new offerings, such as securitized debt. The real estate sector is also expected to formalize, offering institutions access to some domestic deals for the first time.

Despite enormous opportunities, the right entry and exit points in emerging markets still comes with many risks. Signs indicate that investing in just developed markets does not generate the return on the assets secured by institutions, to give investors the best return on their investments. Therefore, it sets the tone for the ability of urban communities to analyse, practice and participate through accounts, savings, and volunteering in these industries that facilitate global and domestic growth which is eventually taxed. At this point they can leverage on the new tax base and create interest and income in their prospective industries and communities, while interest in investors is raised subsequently increasing the GDP.

THE CHALLENGE 4 CHANGE INTIATIVE

Do you want to attract more clients or customers to your business while making a positive difference in the community at the same time? Consider partnering with us, The Challenge 4 Change Initiative (C4CI), *an active approach to utilizing public awareness and adopting measures to reduce crime!*

The Challenge 4 Change Initiative (C4CI) mission is to fight crime through community awareness and education by teaming up with various organizations, law enforcement and government officials (Federal, State and Local), community leaders, entrepreneurs, activists and businesses. The collaboration is geared towards reducing crime and promoting effective prevention strategies and implementation processes.

C4CI defines Crime Prevention as the anticipation, recognition, and appraisal of a crime risk, and the initiation of action to remove or reduce crime. Dedicated to saving lives and creating lasting change in communities, C4CI has implemented a variety of special programs that provide vital tools and resources to empower communities and promote proven crime prevention strategies aimed at creating awareness, encouraging accountability and promoting criminal deterrence. C4CI recognizes that crime prevention and awareness programs work, and are cheaper, safer, and healthier for communities in preventing crime, in comparison to treating victims, dealing with perpetrators, and attending to lost civic health and productivity.

C4CI's community programs include:

1. C4CI's Awareness Program (The C4CI AP Program)

The program enlightens the public about the devastating effects of crime, terms and levels of incarceration, state and grand jury indictments, applicable relevant conduct enhancements at sentencing, pre-sentencing and post-sentencing walk through, and much more.

The program exposes the criminal and judicial system myths, provides intermediate and long-term intervention and counseling tactics, and trains at risk-youth in avoidance techniques directed at creating awareness about escaping from the pitfalls of living a life of crime. C4CI takes a dual approach to crime by focusing on community awareness and education, simultaneously through its awareness and accountability programming. Therefore, without intervention programs such as C4CI, crime victimization rates rise, our communities continue to endure self-destructive patterns of crime, and our businesses bear the unreasonable and unnecessary hikes in taxes to combat crime. If we don't provide our inmates with resources and the skills needed to survive, they will continue to make choices detrimental to themselves and others.

Education and community awareness are keys to helping inmates unlock the shackles of self-hate, destruction and a life of crime. Based on education and awareness, C4CI works to diminish the crime rate and promote early intervention, thus, stimulating the economy through the expansion of businesses.

C4CI programs provide inmates with a fresh start in life by introducing them to new ways of thinking and behaving, ultimately directing them to positive decision-making in their daily lives. Without your help, inmates will remain prisoners of the State, society and themselves. However, when crime prevention is a priority, a strong foundation is laid for future generations as they make wise choices that deter engagement in criminal activities.

HOW YOU CAN HELP:

C4CI is hosting a proactive event aimed at decreasing the number of victims within the business environment and community, while supporting ex-cons aspiring to become a part of society. At C4CI, our neighborhoods can be made safe again, and hope can be restored to those that have been incarcerated. This vision is however not attainable without you. Be a part of the solution and partner with us today by becoming a sponsor, or by making a special donation!

WHY YOUR DONATION IS IMPORTANT:

When you make a donation, you are investing in the lives of our youth and in the safety of the entire community.

Your generous contributions will help us to implement crime prevention programs throughout the state of South Carolina, and aid in creating awareness around crime reduction, lowering of recidivism rates and developing resources for crime victims, families and inmates negatively impacted by the criminal justice system.

Some Alarming Facts...

Crime costs the economy an estimated 500 billion a year! That figure does not include costs to businesses, communities, and families who are the direct victims of the perpetrators of crime. As the cost of crime continues trending upward, the communities, families, and businesses work the hardest and lose the most.

The government's job may be to "protect and serve," but it is not entirely up to them. We all have a part to play. Nearly 1 in every 6 Americans has an encounter with the justice system and the question is will it be you or your loved one?

A distressing statistic indicates that we are only 5% of the world's population but make up 25% of the world's prison population!

It's Time for a Change! Help Us Make a Difference!

Although crime and prisons cost us millions, there is a solution to the problem – Educating criminals. This is a call to educate criminals and the community about the ills crime introduces into the socio-economic space which include unprecedented costs. Additionally, the learning experience reveals little known facts about the 'crime industry'. The value of education is in the contention that crime is a moral and ethical issue perpetuated by ignorance.

We can all strive to reduce the impact of crime by highlighting a unanimous message that crimes are perpetrated by criminals who do not know the ills their crimes create. In this effort we are also able to show how the justice system exaggerates the intent of criminals. Through these efforts we shall shed light on how the community and businesses can win the war against crime by uniting.

Mr. Gallman is currently engaged in forging partnerships with financial companies to help create opportunities for lower income earners participating in the financial sector. Banking on education, development of cashless transactions, asset-based accounts, and long-term high return investment instruments, Gallman hopes to empower families to take control over their financial futures, thereby breaking the cycle of poverty.

Made in the USA
Middletown, DE
03 September 2024

60298610R00071